# He Gave Me Life
*Ruth Spencer*

**Sovereign World**

Therefore with joy shall you draw water out of the wells of salvation

Isaiah 12 v 3

Sovereign World Ltd
P.O. Box 17
Chichester PO20 6RY
England

Bible references are from the New King James Bible ©
Thomas Nelson Publishers Inc, Box 141000, Nashville,
TN 37214, U.S.A. unless otherwise stated.

Bible references marked NASB are from the New
American Standard Bible.
Copyright © The Lockman Foundation 1960, 1962,
1963, 1968, 1971, 1973, 1975, 1977.

Scripture Quotations marked NIV are from the Holy
Bible, New International Version.
Copyright © 1973, 1978, International Bible Society.
Published by Hodder & Stoughton

Scripture Quotations marked RSV are from the Revised
Standard Version. Copyright © Churches of Christ in
the United States of America.

ISBN 1 85240 011 0

Printed and bound in Great Britain by Anchor Brendon
Ltd, Tiptree, Colchester, Essex.

Typeset by M R Reprographics, Chard, Somerset

# Acknowledgements

Thanks to all who helped get this book off the ground. To Canon Jim Glennon who made time in his busy schedule to scan, and write the foreword; to Pastor Frank Houston and Hazel - Frank for the preface and Hazel who scanned, partly edited and also inspired me with a Writers Course; my wonderful children, who have encouraged me to write in spite of the fact that they missed my company: To Margie, my daughter, who designed and painted the cover; to Carol who tip-toed in with cups of tea.

Last, but not least, to my husband Douglas who not only claimed that "The Book" was, in our house, replaced by "the book", or "the book of Ruth", but even contributed by writing the description of the sunset in the final chapter, as well as editing and scanning.

# Dedication

To Jesus, without Whom this book could never have been written, because my life would have been empty, and to the Holy Spirit Who inspired the writing thereof.

# Preface

Ruth Spencer's remarkable story from Egypt, through the Wilderness, to the Promised Land is a revelation of God's love and great grace.

One cannot read this book without realising the truth of God's word.

"My thoughts are not your thoughts, neither are your ways My ways, saith the Lord. For as the heavens are higher than the earth, so are My ways higher than your ways, and My thoughts than your thoughts." Isaiah 55:8,9.

As is the case with so many of us, it is not difficult to see God's hand has been guiding Ruth all through the years. It is not surprising that she is such a strong Christian.

It has been my privilege over the last ten years to work with Ruth and Doug Spencer. They have assisted in building a strong charismatic congregation in the heart of Sydney, Australia's largest city. My wife and I have come to love them dearly.

All who read this inspiring book will undoubtedly be challenged to a greater faith in God. It will be of special benefit to those who are going through their own wilderness experience.

Frank Houston DD,
Senior Pastor
Christian Life Centre, Sydney.

# Foreword

This is a remarkable book written by a remarkable woman. It shows what wonderful things God does for those who put their dependence in Christ and believe in the moment by moment power and guidance of the Holy Spirit.

Ruth Spencer tells the story of her pilgrimage. Its appeal lies in its honesty and its testimony of what God is and does. It is also well written in a simple and graphic style. The reader is carried along from adventure to adventure so there is a sense of anticipation in what is going to happen next.

There is no reason why the reader should not be able to identify with the story of her life in the sense that everyone can have their own version of what Ruth has experienced if only they will respond and walk on the water too. I am pleased to commend her book and hope it will have a wide circulation.

Jim Glennon
Founder of the Healing Ministry in
St. Andrews Cathedral, Sydney.

# The Theme:

The Israelites in the days of Moses left Egypt and, guided by the Holy Spirit were lead through the waste and howling wilderness to the promised land.

This experience is parallelled spiritually in some Christian lives today.

Many a single parent rearing children knows the loneliness of the parched desert, but press on - there is a promised land ahead, as you will read in the following pages.

The events are all true as described, although some names have been altered.

# CONTENTS

| | | Page |
|---|---|---|
| **PART ONE** | **Escape From Egypt** | |
| Chapter 1 | **The Plane Crash** | 21 |
| **PART TWO** | **The Wilderness** | |
| Chapter 2 | **The Journey Begins** | 41 |
| Chapter 3 | **Healings** | 47 |
| | a) Getting to Know Him | |
| Chapter 4 | **Intercession** | 57 |
| Chapter 5 | **Teaching** | 67 |
| Chapter 6 | **Faithbuilders** | 71 |
| | a) The Spoken Word | |
| | b) Trip to Kiama | |
| | c) Gold Stole | |
| | d) May I Go Lord? | |
| | e) Beryl | |
| Chapter 7 | **Growing as Christians** | 75 |
| | a) Giving | |
| | b) Sunday School and Church | |
| | c) Birthday Parties | |
| Chapter 8 | **Incidents Along the Way** | 79 |
| | a) Daddy's Death | |
| | b) Joe | |
| | c) Peter Rabbit | |
| | d) Back to University | |
| Chapter 9 | **Rebellion/Weariness/ Loneliness** | 88 |
| | a) Yohan | |
| | b) Healing of Depression | |
| | c) Parting with Yohan | |

# PART THREE THE PROMISED LAND

Chapter 10    **Crossing Jordan**    97
a) Baptism in the Holy Spirit
b) Repentance
c) Rebellion
d) Water Baptism

Chapter 11    **My Jericho**    107
a) Affliction - I Need a Man

Chapter 12    **Visit to Israel**    109
a) Kathryn Kuhlman

Chapter 13    **Battles and Blessings**    116
a) Sealed Orders
b) Crisis Call
c) Demon Possession
d) Fellowship Group
e) Occult
f) Death Wish
g) Kihilla
h) Parable of "Ruth "
i) Douglas Joins Crisis Call

Chapter 14    **Town Hall Healing**    129

Chapter 15    **A New Marriage**    131
a) Honeymoon
b) Upper room Anointing

Chapter 16    **Prophecy Fulfilled**    137

Chapter 17    **Healing (Slipped Disc)**    139

Chapter 18    **A New Church**    141
a) Wave of Revival
b) Crisis Call Handed Over

Chapter 19    **More Blessings**    144
a) U.S.A. Trip
b) Lost Luggage
c) Counselling
d) Healing (Knees)

| Chapter 20 | **God Speaks At Goulburn** | 149 |
| Chapter 21 | **Our Mission To Moscow** | 153 |
| | a) The Vision | |
| | b) The Preparation | |
| | c) The Provision | |
| | d) The Journey Begins | |
| | e) Honolulu | |
| | f) Japan | |
| | g) Incident at the Border | |
| | h) The Trans Siberian Railway | |
| | i) Moscow | |
| | j) To Leningrad and the Border | |
| | k) The Persecuted Church | |
| | l) What can we do to help the Russian Church? | |
| Chapter 22 | **Healing (Bowel)** | 204 |
| Chapter 23 | **Mummy's Death** | 206 |
| Chapter 24 | **Music** | 209 |
| Chapter 25 | **Rain** | 214 |
| Chapter 26 | **Further Back Healing** | 220 |
| Chapter 27 | **The Burma (or Death) Railway** | 221 |
| | a) Bob Halliday - A Friend in Need | |
| | b) Bob's Story | |
| | c) Jesus the Answer | |
| | d) James and Annie, Missionaries to Malaysia | |

| Chapter 28 | **Feast of Tabernacles** | 230 |
| | a) Release of the Soviet Jews | |
| | b) The Second Exodus | |
| Chapter 29 | **Return of the Jews to Israel** | 234 |
| Chapter 30 | **We Visit the Burma Railway** | 239 |
| | a) Benaiah James | |
| Chapter 31 | **Guidance or Divination?** | 243 |
| Chapter 32 | **Christ in You - The Hope of Glory** | 245 |
| Chapter 33 | **Writing This Book** | 248 |
| Chapter 34 | **Living it all Again** | 250 |

# PART ONE

# Escape From Egypt

# Chapter 1
# The Plane Crash

"Mummy, when is Daddy coming home?"

The question I dreaded for weeks had now been asked, and I must reply. How do you tell a little boy of three that his daddy is dead?

My heart was aching as I said "Darling, Daddy won't be coming home, he had an accident, he was hurt badly, he died......he's gone to live in Heaven with God."

How my heart groaned within me. I had become reconciled to Bob's death myself, it was some months ago now, but James must know that the daddy he loved so much would not be back. He'd left our lives forever.

"Where's Heaven mummy?"

"God, please help me, how do I make him understand?"

My mind flashed back to the fateful night of November ninth, 1957, when I discovered that the plane, a four-engined Pan Am Super-Constellation on which Bob was a passenger, was missing, and I realised with horror that it had probably crashed. Radio contact had ceased.

Many strange events preceded and accompanied the crash, and later I could trace the hand of God in it all, but at this stage I was completely oblivious to anything like that.

Bob and I had been married ten years before, and finally settled in a waterfrontage home at Kangaroo Point, with our three children - two girls and a boy, Lindsay, Julia and James, and another on the way.

Bob and I would spend our Saturdays in the boat fishing and relaxing, while Mrs. Murray the baby-sitter minded the children. It was a wonderful way of unwinding. Bob's week as General Manager of a printing firm was pressured, and mine equally demanding, looking after the children aged at this time between three and eight. However, unanswered questions were stirring in my heart.

I remember sitting fishing for flathead and thinking "What has life to offer? What are my goals? What's it all about? Surely life is not about material gain - I've got most things now - a loving husband, three lovely children and another soon to be born, a car of my own. What have I to reach out for? There must be something. Life can't be this shallow."

About four months before his death, Bob and I were talking. Suddenly he said "What is your particular Philosophy?" I hardly knew what the word meant, but of course wouldn't admit this.

"Well, if everyone was nice to everyone else, a sort of 'love your neighbour' policy, the world would be a happier place," I told him. "What a wishy-washy outlook on life. I believe we are here to have children. Perhaps one of them will do something wonderful for the world like inventing penicillin", Bob said.

I felt in my heart this was wrong too, so I bought a book on Philosophy, which I intended to read on a forthcoming trip to Melbourne.

The book left me cold until I came to the chapter on "The Soul and Immortality". There the word "God" was written. Immediately my heart quickened. "I don't want Philosophy, I want God".

On the Melbourne trip, while having drinks one night with Bob and his friend Michael, I asked Mike "If God is good, and everything He made is good, who made the Devil?" He was a Catholic, so I felt he would know all the biblical answers. Mike carefully explained about Lucifer, and his fall.

Bob said later "This bloke Christ really lived, you know". He reminded me that it was about time the children received some religious instruction. "What good will that do them?" I replied. "Let them grow up and make up their own minds. Let's not thrust religion on them."

When we returned home I began reading the New Testament for the first time in my life. As soon as I heard anyone coming I used to hide it under a cushion. Bob referred to 'Bible Bashers', and I didn't want to be classified as one. I thought, "When I go to hospital to have the baby I'll take the Bible and read it and I don't care if the nurses think I'm crazy. I want to know about God."

And so I packed the Bible amongst my maternity things and after Margaret was born, and I was being wheeled down to my room just before midnight, I thought "Thank God, now I'll be able to read without fear of ridicule."

I read Matthew, Mark, Luke and half of John in hospital, little realising that God was preparing me for the coming tragedy in my life.

Two weeks before Bob left on his fateful trip, I came across a large envelope containing photos. I drew one out - a large photo of a coffin covered with the Australian flag. My heart sank, and I said "Oh no", and pushed it back in the package. It was the photograph of Donnie's funeral. Donnie was my fiancé. During the war he was killed in armoury practice in Wirraway in Canada.

I turned very bitter against God through his death. Like many 20-year olds I was afraid he might die. Many pilots were killed about this time in the Battle for Britain, and over Germany. I did what I thought was the best thing for him. I went to Church every Sunday for six months, to pray for him. When he was killed I was angry. I said "God, You obviously don't answer prayer, so in future I'm not attending Church. I'm not praying, and I'm living my life how I choose." I didn't enter a church for fifteen years, except for my marriage to Bob, and the christening of our children and godchildren. That was mainly out of superstition and tradition.

The sight of the coffin disturbed me, but I thrust it from my mind.

Margie was only one month old when Bob said "I would like to take you away on a holiday before I go abroad. You might not have a break for a long time, and I'd like to be with you alone for a while." We took a week's holiday in Melbourne, enjoying one another's company.

A few days before he left Bob was saying goodbye to Mrs. Murray. "Be sure you come back with lots of money" she said, and Bob jokingly answered "I'll only come back with lots of money if I'm dead." He had taken out a large Insurance Policy, which he handed to me saying "This will provide for you and the children if I don't come back." I threw it unceremoniously on the sideboard, saying "Thanks, I'd rather have you." Bob retrieved it. "No, be sensible, keep it somewhere safe, it's a long way to fly."

Premonition? He had never done anything like this on previous overseas trips.

On the day he left I waved goodbye with James' hand in mine. As he strode up the path to the gate I cried "God, please bring him back". The song on my heart at the time was a popular one. "Love is a bird that folds its wings and flies away." As the tears ran down my cheeks I thought "This is ridiculous, we've

24

been married ten years, and I'm still in love with my husband."

Almost as soon as Bob left, Lindsay came out in spots. Chickenpox. The others including the baby caught them. When we were just recovering from this, Julia got Mumps. I was worried about James catching Mumps because he was a delicate child, and when Bob rang from England I told him about this and said "Please hurry home."

In the last few months I was drawn back to God again. Each night I would say the Lord's Prayer, but when I came to "Forgive us our trespasses as we forgive those who trespass against us", I felt hypocritical because I'd had a "falling out" with the lady across the road. It was all over dogs - hers and ours.

She had a little dog and we had a big aggressive dalmation who loved to fight. One day he went across the road and bit her little silky terrier putting it into hospital. The day it came home he went over and bit it in exactly the same place, putting it back into hospital. She told us to keep our dog locked up, which was fair enough, but it was difficult as there were no fences in our section of Kangaroo Point. I bought a muzzle, but we couldn't keep it on him. Bob had refused to keep him locked in the laundry, and I was at a loss as to what to do. She and I hadn't spoken for about two years.

The night before the crash she was playing cricket with her son, and he hit a ball which landed at my feet as I locked the garage. I thought "If she comes over after the ball I'll make up this quarrel." She did. We chatted and became good friends again.

As I walked down the path to the house I thought "Thank God, I'll be able to say my prayers tonight without feeling a hypocrite." I realised later that God was putting me in a state of grace, as it were, because

25

soon I would be praying more desperately than ever before in my life.

The next day was Saturday and Mrs. Murray was coming to help with the children. Heavy depression began settling on me, and I was so unsure of myself I couldn't even cross the street where I was shopping. When I finally arrived home I said "Mrs. Murray, I feel so depressed I just don't care if he never comes home."

That night my sister Jean rang asking when Bob was due home as her husband hoped to meet him at the airport.

"Jean, I'm so depressed, I haven't heard from him since he's been in the USA, and I feel he may have met with an accident."

I hung up the phone and sat there plunged into a dark sort of daydream. In it Bob said to me "I'm leaving you, and I'm taking James." Bob moved towards the stairs, and I thought "How will I stop him?" The first thing that came to hand was a hammer I had in the kitchen, so I hit Bob on the back of the head and he fell. I realised I'd hit him too hard, and he was dead.

The dream passed but I felt absolutely shocked. This was a premonition of death. I lay down on my bed and fell into a deep sleep. As I slept, Bob died. That was the exact time of the crash.

When I awoke about an hour later the dreadful depression had lifted. I was light and happy. "Mrs. Murray, I'm so excited, I feel Bob may come home tonight."

At about 10pm the phone rang. Someone wanted information about a William Holiday who was flying Pan Am between San Fransisco and Honolulu. "That's strange" I said. "My husband Robert Halliday may be on that flight. If you find he is on the plane will you please let me know?" After he hung up I thought "That's funny. If they wanted Holiday how did they get on to Halliday?" Suspicions aroused, I rang Pan Am, and asked if there was anything amiss.

"Yes", said Pan Am, "a plane is down, but it has effected a surface landing. The lights are on, and it is floating nicely. By now rescue ships will be leaving Honolulu. This also happened a few months ago, the passengers got onto the plane's wing, and the most severe injury was a bruised knee."

The front doorbell rang at 10.45pm. Reporters and cameramen from one of the evening papers crowded around. I refused to speak to them because of the in-humane way in which they approached me. Besides, I wasn't very concerned at this stage, because the plane was "floating nicely" with its lights on. "Lucky Bob", I thought. "All the exciting things happen to him. Wish I were there too," and went to sleep.

About 3am I rang Pan Am to make sure the passengers were rescued, only to find that the "Plane floating nicely with its lights on" was an ocean freighter, and there was no sign of the missing aircraft. ...... But there was an oil slick where the plane had obviously sunk, and a dye marker, which could have exploded when the plane sank. It could have been dropped by a raft if the passengers were on rafts, which was now hoped. A dye marker marks the spot for searching planes, and acts as a shark repellant. There was no wreckage. If a plane explodes or crash lands, the sea is usually covered with pieces of the plane for an area of a couple of miles, depending on the violence of the crash.

I rang Bob's mother and my people about 4.30am because the Sunday papers are delivered early in some areas. By now I had realised the seriousness of the situation and was cold with shock. I had to wear an overcoat in the house, although the weather was warm. A few days later at least half of my hair also fell out.

All Sunday we waited for news.

On Monday I saw a minister of religion walking down the front steps. He had a back-to-front collar on and I just froze. He looked to me like the personification of death, and I didn't want to let him in the house. However, rather than be rude, I took him downstairs to the children's room.

He was a lovely young man who said he had been led by the Lord to visit me. I'd never darkened the doorway of his church, but the whole front page of the newspapers was taken up with "The Missing Plane". Bob was the only Australian on board, and he could see by our address that we were in his parish.

He read me Psalm 27:

v1. "The Lord is my light and my salvation, whom shall I fear? The Lord is the strength of my life, of whom shall I be afraid?"

v14. "Wait on the Lord, be of good courage and He shall strengthen your heart, wait I say on the Lord."

He said "You must have faith."

"How can I have faith, my husband may already be dead?"

"You must have HOPE he is alive, and FAITH in God if he is dead."

To me having faith meant that he was alive, but I was prepared to go along with this attitude and said "I will have hope he is alive and until someone shows that he must assuredly be dead, like producing his body, I will not acknowledge his death. If he is dead, I will have faith in God.

"Wait on the Lord, be of good courage and He shall strengthen your heart". The scripture stayed in my mind. I will be of good courage, and He will strengthen me. If I throw up my hands and say "I can't go on" He can't strengthen that, I will be of good courage.

The minister then prayed with me, but the main thing I remember was that my cigarette was burning my fingers, and I hoped he'd hurry and finish.

My mother was staying with me to help with the baby until we heard the outcome of the crash. The Radio reported "Today Mrs. Halliday received a letter from her husband who is on the missing plane." A couple of hours later the letter arrived at my home. How on earth the Media knew this I will never know. It began "My dear Wife", and I remembered the letter I received after Donnie's death fifteen years before. I served in the WAAAF, and he called me his "Wiffy WAAAffey Wifey". This had become shortened to "dear Wifey". My heart sank. He's dead! But I still wouldn't allow myself to believe this.

S.O.S. signals were then picked up on the International Distress Frequency and I thought "Thank God, they'll be able to take a bearing, and the rafts will soon be found." I was a Direction-finding Operator in WAAAF Signals during the war, and remembered how we plotted a plane's course by radio beam. "It's just a matter of time, and they'll be rescued!"

We waited all day.

Then, the following day, we were told there were no more signals, but they'd sighted a flare! My mother, who was not an outgoing Christian, said to me "Let's kneel down and thank God that they will soon be found." Awkwardly we got to our knees and prayed.

When my mother was not with me, my mother-in-law hovered in the background, never quite out of sight. I realised later she thought I might be suicidal, and felt I should be watched day and night. Nothing was further from my mind, but in retrospect I am so pleased she was there, even though I was irritated at the time. I feel she saved me from something really bad.

My grandmother on the paternal side was a Spiritualist Medium, right into the Occult, and I inherited some of her mediumistic powers. I had two premonitions of death. The first was of Donnie's death during the war, when I sat up in bed at 2am and wrote to him saying "I feel there is something wrong, please write", just at the time he was killed over in Canada, and later felt his presence in the room. I was frightened and ran in to my parents, spending the rest of the night in bed with my mother.

Now it was Bob's. I was trying to tune in to Bob on the raft, to contact his psyche, and know he was alive. I was irritated because my mother-in-law wouldn't leave me to my spiritual projections, but am relieved now, because I was in danger of contacting occult powers which undoubtedly would have deceived me and drawn me into their dark realm. God is good.

The flare turned out to be dropped from one of the searching planes. Now there was silence, a terrible silence There was even talk of calling off the search.

By this time, three or four days had passed since the crash. The main item of news was "Is the dog in Sputnik still alive?" The forty-four people on the plane, a four engined aircraft, included seven children, but they took second place to the dog which was the first living creature sent into orbit by the Russians. It was one of the cruel stabbings of fate. I began to dislike the poor animal, doomed to a lonely death in space. Let's get our priorities right.

By now I had learned Psalm 27 by heart, I could lie on my bed and meditate on that and the Lord's Prayer. They comforted me. I tried to read another Psalm, but found that in times of shock our minds just can't cope with anything extra. I realise it is so important to stock our minds with God's Word while everything is going well.

I was so thankful for the readings I'd had in Hospital when God was preparing me for this shock. I remembered how Jesus had raised Lazarus from the dead after four days. I prayed to Jesus and told Him that I believed He could still have Bob found - on a life raft, even floating on a piece of plane's wing if it was His will. I was a bit uncomfortable praying to Jesus in case God was jealous, but risked it and asked Him to forgive me if I'd done anything wrong, My idea of God at this stage was the Father alone.

My mind went back to an article I'd read in "Religion and Life". It was about a Minister who claimed he had been in the Ministry for twelve years before he "had found Christ", and what a difference it had made to his ministry. I couldn't understand this but prayed "Christ, if You can make any difference in this case, please do it." Because I couldn't understand it I thrust the thought back into the files of my mind.

On Wednesday I asked the Minister when he arrived "Who is the Holy Ghost?" He replied "The Holy Ghost is the great Comforter". I couldn't understand this either, so pushed it back in my mind as well.

All this time I had been wonderfully upheld by God. I was in a state where, even though it seemed every hour or so there was a fresh twist to the knife in my heart, the pain was eased by a growing faith in God. He had promised He would strengthen my heart, and He was doing just that.

Admiral Nimitz, in charge of the American Fleet based in Hawaii believed the forty-four passengers could still be alive on the rafts. He ordered the whole fleet out to sea to help in the search. They swept a lane

200 miles wide on the plane's course between Honolulu and San Francisco.

On Friday night, some hours before the bodies were found, I began to feel as though I couldn't go much longer without collapsing. I locked the door of my bedroom and began to call out to God. I realised I had no grounds on which to approach Him. I'd never done anything for Him, so I couldn't say "God, I did this for You, please have Bob found, dead or alive."

At this point I saw the whole of my life pass quickly before me. "It's wasted, my life is wasted, not a single thing for God." I cried, I was desolate. I knew God could hear me, but there seemed no way I could get through to him. A big cloud existed between us. It was a cloud of my sin, my selfishness. He could hear me, but there was no earthly reason why He should do anything for me.

Clenching my fists in desperation I pummelled on the wall calling out "O God, hear me". I turned and was half way over to the bed when suddenly I felt His presence in the room. I stopped still. I couldn't even feel my feet touching the floor, as a beautiful peace and love and healing power flowed through me. There was a stillness - the presence of God. My hands, which had been shaking with emotion, were now steady, and as I noticed this, I heard the Voice of God speak audibly to me.

"Holy Ghost".

He had answered my question "Who is the Holy Ghost?" It was a perfectly modulated Voice, heard not with my ears, or in my head, but in my diaphragm. I later learned that the Ancients used to call this the "Seat of the Soul".

I stood stock still. In time to come I'll think I was over-wraught and imagined the Voice, so I'm not moving till I know in my heart that I am sane, and that

I heard the voice of another Person. I also feel wonderful, totally healed.

I've been wasting my time, if God can do this He can do anything. I knew that the Bible said we have three score years and ten, and that I was now thirty four and a half, almost half way. I've spent half my life for myself, I'll spend the rest of my life for God.

The wonderful presence and healing of the Lord filled me and lifted me into a new realm of peace. He alone knew that within hours the bodies would be recovered, and Bob indeed proved to be dead, but as Psalm 91:4 says "He shall cover you with His feathers, and under His wings you shall take refuge", and I snuggled close to Him.

The following morning Pan Am rang and told me the news before I could hear it over the radio. The whole story was starkly revealed in the morning papers. The American Fleet had found the bodies, twenty of them, some still strapped to their seats, all wearing life jackets. They had been swept eighty eight miles under the sea by the strong ocean currents and had taken six days to surface. The bodies, mercifully including Bob's, had been picked up by one of the Aircraft Carriers and were being ferried back to Long Beach, California. Bob's self-winding Omega watch still ticked, telling the correct time.

I was so thankful that his body was recovered. Bob was such a strong personality I almost felt that even if the plane blew up, it could never hurt him. I wasn't the only one who felt like this. One of his friends said exactly the same thing to me when we were waiting for news. I think I would have still wondered if he were alive somewhere, and would turn up years later like Enoch Arden.

Bob had said to me months previously when he asked what my philosophy was "If I could choose my death I would drown, it's a good clean death."

God upheld me through all this horror, but I feel every vestige of emotion was drained from me. I thought "If someone were to chop a person to small pieces before my eyes I wouldn't flinch. I could watch it all without feeling." I later found that my emotions were so shocked that when I wanted to laugh I would cry, and when I wanted to cry I'd laugh. It was as though I walked in a dream, but this was God's way of keeping me sane.

The bodies were taken to Long Beach, California. We wanted Bob's body cremated and the ashes flown back, but this was not acceptable. We had to fly someone over to identify his body. He was then carried home - in a bronze coffin. Arrangements had to be made for transfer to a wooden coffin for cremation. I wouldn't allow anyone else to make the arrangements as I loved him so much, and wanted to do this last thing for him myself.

When the Death Certificate came, it showed that the principal cause of death was the extensive basal skull fracture - just exactly where I dreamed I'd hit him with a hammer.

The Death Certificate and our Marriage Certificate had one strange thing in common - each was dated the 8th and this was crossed out and the 9th inserted. Our Marriage Certificate was incorrectly dated 8th, a line drawn through the 9th written beside it, whereas on the Death Certificate he died the other side of the International Date Line, 8th there and 9th here. God was showing me he knew the date and conditions of Bob's death the day we were married ten and a half years previously. I realise now, if not then, God knows all things, the end from the beginning.

Two and a half weeks after his death the funeral took place. As the Minister began his eulogy, a jet plane screamed down over the funeral parlour as a reminder of the crash. I'd never attended a funeral before, and here before me was the coffin, draped with a flag (at his mother's request), just as I had seen it a few weeks before in Donnie's photo. I gazed at the coffin in shocked unbelief. Was the one I loved so dearly lying white and still in that box? My eyes were glued to it all through the service. Then I found I had to walk down the aisle behind it as the box was carried out. Something in me died at that time.

One of the sympathy letters we received said that love was like a bird that sometimes flies away. I was reminded of the song I was singing the day he left "Love is a bird that folds its wings and flies away." The name of the plane was "Romance of the Skies".

During this traumatic time my spiritual life was changing rapidly. I had now come into the realisation that God was a personal God Who really loved me. I honestly thought that if I wrote to the newspapers and told them I'd heard the Voice of God that everybody in Sydney would turn to Him. How naive!

I remembered with concern the awful feeling of being estranged from God and determined that would never happen to me again. But how could I make sure of remaining in His favour? How about the bad things I'd done? Two sins in particular plagued me. One was an abortion I had had years ago, a great sadness and guilt in my life. How could I be forgiven for such a horrendous act? What on earth could I do to atone for this tragedy?

As yet I hadn't discussed my new-found faith with anyone, not even the minister. I tried to reason things out for myself. I thought, incorrectly, "God the Father sent His Son Jesus down to this earth to show us how He wants us to live. If I live by His teachings given in the Sermon on the Mount, the Ten Command ments etc., surely the Father will be pleased with me and after a few years may say "Well done Ruth. You've been a good girl for a few years now. I'll just forget about those few bad things you've done". It was like sweeping them under the mat. I didn't realise that God doesn't work that way.

"I'll buy a big new Bible, one with large print. I'll be reading it for the rest of my life, so I'll get one that won't strain my eyes," and off I went to town, to the Salvation Army Bookshop. When I asked for the largest Bible they had they produced a Lectern Bible, so large it can only be read comfortably resting on a table.

I rang Bob's Aunt. "Belle, I've become interested in God, would you come over some time and tell me about Him?" Belle and Uncle Stan came. Stan played with the children while Belle told me about her faith. "The Person you need is Jesus. He is so wonderful. He heals today as He did when he walked here on earth. We have wonderful healings at Christ Church. You need Jesus ."

I was envious. "Isn't that wonderful she talks about Him as though she knows Him. Wouldn't it be wonderful to know Him like that".

The children had received no Christian instruction, and so I had been reading a Bible story to them each night before they went to bed, and on finishing that book read the child's version of "Pilgrim's Progress" Pilgrim set out from the City of Destruction to journey to Mt. Zion, carrying a great pack of "sins" on his back. He struggled through the Slough of Despond, laboriously climbed the hill and at the top knelt at the foot of the Cross, where the bundle of sins on his back rolled down a hole at the foot of the Cross (the Sepulchre), and he leaped to his feet, a free man.

Pilgrim shouted for joy "Not a sin to my name", and as I read this the Lord seemed to say, "Where are your sins?" Strangely enough I couldn't remember what they were. I thought "This is ridiculous", because they had been heavy on me, but now they were gone. I had to sit down and think before I could remember what they were.

About this time Paul, the minister, arrived to invite me to Bible Study. His wife Christine was at home praying that I'd receive Jesus as Saviour. I told Paul what the Lord had been doing in my life, and he said "Wait till I go home and bring a couple of little booklets which will explain things better than I can", and raced off, returning with "Justification" and "Sanctification". They explained that one didn't have to work one's way into God's favour, indeed one could not, but Jesus took our sins on the Cross and was offering me free pardon. By His grace, His unmeritted favour, my sins were forgiven as I handed my life over to Him as Saviour and Lord. I saw that like Pilgrim I didn't have a sin to my name. Thirty four and a clean slate, wow!

With Jesus, God had given me the Holy Spirit, Eternal Life, and my name was written in the "Book of Life". If I died tonight I would go to Heaven. Hallelujah!

Christine asked "Did she give her heart to the Lord?" Paul said "She's a Christian already but she doesn't know it." The Holy Spirit had been working steadily and surely in my life, separating me to Himself. I was now a child of God, set apart to Him. Gone were my old standards. A new life had begun.

About this time my father bought me a house near his. With the help of my parents and some friends we moved from Kangaroo Point to Lindfield. The home was a wonderful provision of the Lord, through my generous father.

God provided for me in many ways so that I was financially secure and mercifully didn't have to work to support the family. Lindsay and Julia settled happily into their new school. That was great, for they'd been bringing up their breakfast every morning for about six weeks.

There was a large sunny playing area at our new home, with a tennis court. It was used for bikes and soccer and everything but tennis.

With plenty of children in the neighbourhood we had up to ten or twelve some days, so for the children the terrible blow of losing daddy was softened by the happiness of their new surroundings.

This new life, this wonderful Jesus, was overwhelming to one so used to living in the world. Jesus promised to be a Husband to me, the Father of my fatherless children. Nevertheless, my heart still ached for Bob, and his arms about me. If only I could share all this with him.

With tears I recalled a portion of a poem learned years before at school:

"Oh for the touch of a vanished hand, and the sound of a voice that is still".

Egypt, the old life, was behind me.

# PART TWO

# The Wilderness

# Chapter 2
# The Journey Begins

The trauma of moving from the family home at Kangaroo Point is still indelibly etched in my mind. The emptiness of it all, the heartache of remembering what was, and now was not. The break-up of a family is a tragedy, be it through death or divorce.

I wandered around the property sadly making plans for the move. What would I do with the boat, drifting idly on its mooring? I could see Bob there with his fishing tackle busy coiling ropes. I could hear the motor starting up. No, I mustn't listen, mustn't visualise these things - they have gone forever. I couldn't face the thought of selling the boat which was so much part of our lives. I gave it away.

The cradle and winch and slips which Bob and I built together must remain. I remember wading in the George's River carrying one end of the railway sleepers with Bob on the other end. Our feet sank deep into the mud as we prepared to lay the slips. Every step was an effort, not only with the weight of the sleepers, but the suction as well. As one tries to lift one's feet out of deep thick mud, the effort is incredible.

The railway lines we used as slips were also heavy. They were laid on the sleepers and sledge hammered into position with cleats. What a lot of fun, but hard work.

No, I mustn't remember. I must forget these things that are past, and press on.

What should I do with Bob's tools under the house? His crowbar, pick and shovel, sledge hammer and other things useless to women, like heavy axes and two-handed saws? Then there were the ladders, the children's swing and see-saw. They must all be taken.

The dog! Pots, (the Dalmation), the family friend, so called because Lindsay said "Look at his li'l pots" when we first bought him as a pup, what was to become of Pots? In times past he lay faithfully beside the basinette of each child, growling at any stranger who approached.

Pots was old. He had survived three cancer operations, but the Vet agreed that he'd come to the end of the road. He had caused me so much trouble with the neighbours in the past I just couldn't face more at our new home.

In tears I hugged him in a final goodbye, and he responded with the usual tailwag and the strange twisted smile only he could give. (He did this by curling his mouth up over his teeth in a grimace which we called his smile.) Poor Pots! Even you must suffer at this time. I handed him over to the Vet and walked away. The empty kennel haunted me each time I walked past. It was another twist of the knife.

Another wrench came leaving the garden with all the precious little unusual plants we'd cared for in the natural rockery, the tree ferns etc. It hurt to leave them. The house would be unoccupied for some months till probate was passed. They would probably die. So many things dying around me, help me to go on Lord.

I had repainted the bedroom as a surprise for Bob, in the latest strong colours. The bedhead wall and bed I painted dark mountain blue, the cupboards and wall burgundy and the other two walls grey. It was striking with silver bed lamps. I'd dyed the Indian carpet to match the walls.

Now instead of proudly showing him my work, I was confronted by all Bob's clothes hanging in his cupboard. Only one who has wept their way through the belongings of a lost loved one would understand the grief. God, help me. The Salvation Army was helpful and collected things. Now the empty cupboard looked even worse.

And then the boxes! In the confusion I forgot to write a list of the contents on the outside.

"Mummy where is......?" "In one of the boxes". "Which one?" "I don't know". Then a frantic unloading of things onto the floor.

I think perhaps my parents minded the children the day the furniture vans arrived, I don't remember. But I do remember taking down the sign swinging by the front gate.... "THE HALLIDAYS", "No 38". It would never be used again now that the leading Halliday was gone.

When the long drive to our new home at Lindfield - a haven, a shelter from the storm, where we began our new life.

When we first arrived at Lindfield I put all our beds on the verandah, pushed close together in a line. Firstly my double bed, flanked by the basinette and James's cot, then the two single beds for Lindsay and Julia. I was hoping to give the children a feeling of security and togetherness. The moon made strange shadows through the trees. Sleep was impossible, so we moved into the house. I occupied the bedroom with James and the baby, Julia and Lindsay were in the second.

I was awakened by two frightened girls running down the hall to my room. "Mummy, there's a tiger outside our window." We'd never owned a cat, only a dog who kept them well away, and the girls had heard this loud yowling cat-fight right outside their window. I explained, chased the cats away, and tucked them both back into bed.

It was now December. Somehow we survived that first Christmas without Bob. The Lord upheld us in our sadness. I remember little about that Christmas except that the children had made friends with the neighbours and seemed happy.

It is a lonely thing rearing children without their daddy. There are so many times when I longed to say "Look darling, she's cut her first tooth, look darling, she's walking, look at James riding his bike, look at this school report, Julia is doing so well, Lindsay is dancing with three other girls on Speech Day" etc.

Sometimes I pretended I heard Bob's car in the drive or heard him putting his key in the lock of the front door. This was fantasy, and wrong. However, Jesus was with us and gave me wonderful Bible promises for the children.

"All your children shall be taught by the Lord, and great shall be the peace of your children."
Isaiah 54:13

"Fear not.... I will pour My Spirit on your descendants, and My blessing on your offspring; they will spring up among the grass like willows by the watercourses......Another will call himself by the name of Jacob."            Isaiah 44:3-5
(James is a contraction of Jacob.)

"For your Maker is your husband, the Lord of Hosts is His name."            Isaiah 54:5

The wonderful comfort of the Holy Spirit encompassed me.

My new friends Paul and Christine were kindness itself to the family. They made themselves available day and night to help, and gradually I found my feet. For the first few weeks I lived in an emotionless world, known only by people who have been bereaved. From being full, life becomes so unbearably empty.

When Donnie was killed it had been the same. I remember looking out the window at people walking past. People who were laughing and talking. "How can the sun shine, the birds sing, people laugh, in fact the world go on as usual, when my heart is breaking?"

I remember how I lost the will to live, how that within a day or two of learning of Donnie's death I slipped mounting a horse, just lay across the saddle, the horse cantering off. I slid under its hoofs thinking at the same time "I don't care if I die, I rather hope I do."

I was a WAAAF at Richmond Air Base at the time, during the War, and didn't have the heart to join in any dances etc. till my room-mate Cecily took me in hand and said "Be sensible, you are alive and he is dead. Nothing will bring him back, but you must get on with living." This advice from Cecily years ago helped me adjust now.

So in our new-found faith we took heart, and began to grow.

I remember the sign the Lord gave me within two weeks of Bob's funeral. Margie was christened at the little church near Kangaroo Point, and from the time of the ceremony (which was sad because Bob's absence was so terribly obvious), there was a large star in the sky. I have never before or since seen a star in broad daylight, and knew in my heart that Jesus was saying "I love you, I love the baby. From now on I will shower blessings upon the family, this is My promise to you." The star was visible for about half an hour, but did not appear the following day.

We began to grow in faith, and the children came to know God in a real way. Lindsay and Julia asked Jesus into their hearts when the Wordless Book was read to them, as James did when he was five. When I told him his sins were forgiven he said "What happens if I sin again?" A child can be "Born Again" by the Spirit incredibly young. Margie too received Jesus at five, but being independent, waited till Mum was out of the room before asking Christine to pray with her.

Margie was only three months old when her father died, and I had five years at home in which to study before she started school. The day began at 6am with the baby's morning feed. For the first time in my life I rose at 4.30am each morning and read the Bible till 6am, and in this way God gave me an overall picture from Genesis to Revelation, reading approximately twelve or thirteen chapters a morning, to get the feel of the Book.

# Chapter 3
# Healings

The wonderful answers to prayer helped faith grow. Each night the children had been praying for a little boy, Stuart, whose abdominal organs were outside his body at birth. The children had never met him, but years later when names were called out for Polio Injections, he was seated next to us in the Health Centre, as large as life and to all appearances in perfect health.

At bedtime the children and I would pray for people and circumstances on our hearts. I had read where hurricanes in the West Indies and islands off Florida, USA, had cost the lives of up to 2000 or 3000 people. On two occasions we prayed that hurricanes bearing down upon Florida be diverted. Both changed course and there was no loss of life and little material damage.

On another occasion we prayed at each meal over the weekend that the road toll would be reduced. On TV the announcer said "This weekend has been most unusual. There have been no deaths on the NSW roads."

We were learning to walk by faith. As anyone knows who tries to walk this path, eventually the Lord asks if one has faith for healing. I was nervous about this as Bob and I had spent a small fortune on doctor's fees for James. I made a decision "Yes Lord, I'll trust You for our health." Soon the Medical Benefits Insurance was due for payment. "Seeing you are trusting Me for your health, you won't need to renew this will you?" Fear rose within, but I said "No, I'll trust You Lord."

Then James had another bout of tonsillitis. He usually convulsed when his temperature rose above 102°. I panicked. "Lord, if his temperature rises above 102° I'll have to call the doctor." That afternoon up it went past danger level. I rang the Doctor and asked him to come down urgently. He hurried down and prescribed antibiotics and disprin to reduce the temperature. That night my Bible reading was from Kings, speaking of King Asa "Asa became diseased in his feet, and his malady was very severe; yet in his disease he did not seek the Lord, but the physicians." 2 Chron 16:12 Wow! Forgive my lack of faith Lord. After this our visits to the doctor were rare, but Jesus gave us wonderful health.

Once James's headmaster called and said "I think James has broken his wrist. He jumped over the garbage tin and caught his foot on the lid. He crashed on the asphalt and caught his arm underneath him. You'll probably have to take him to have it X-rayed." I knelt to pray about it before going to the school and the Lord gave me Psalm 22 to read, in which it says "I can count all my bones" (meaning that they are sound.) In other words "Not one of His bones shall be broken". John 19:36.

A strange dialogue took place at the school. "Are you taking him to have the wrist X-rayed?" "No, it's not broken." "How do you know?" "The Lord told me". The headmaster looked at me incredulously. Sure enough, the wrist was totally healed in a few days.

I had many testings over James's health. Once when he had a very sore throat, the infection travelled up into his ear drums. One ear began discharging. From that awful day of testing he didn't have another ear problem, and his hearing is perfect. Thankyou Jesus.

I prayed for the children and took them to bed with me when they were sick. Generally by the morning they were better.

The healings were marvellous really. I slipped a disc and was in much pain for a few days. Margaret, aged four, was normally a very gentle girl. Suddenly she ran towards me while I was talking to a friend, and pushed me on the hip with all her might. I fell sideways, and the disc went straight back - a perfect manipulation, thankyou Lord.

A friend, June, was rushed to hospital with an acute asthma attack. As I was leaving home to visit her, the Lord gave the reading "And He touched her and healed her." Often we feel quite threatened about touching another person, and I said, almost apologetically, "June, I feel the Lord asked me to touch you and you will be healed. Do you mind?" Of course June didn't mind She really was longing for someone to put their arm around her and love and comfort her. I touched her arm gingerly and prayed, and by the following morning she was healed and home.

Touching is one of the ways we transmit love. Why are we so reticent? A mother strokes and caresses her child when it is hurt. Why can't we love one another like this?

James, only five or six, had a blockage in the urinary tract, and through high temperatures and dehydration, was forming uric-acid crystals, or stones. The crystals were removed by urgent operation, but there seemed to be one lodged in the kidney. He screamed with pain. The doctors decided he should have a kidney dye test the following day. I read Mark 11:24.

"Whatever things you ask when you pray, believe that you receive them, and you will have them."

I prayed this way "Thankyou Lord, I believe You are healing him. I believe there is no blockage in the kidneys and he is totally healed."

I hopped into bed, fell asleep with James beside me. Some time later I wakened with a wonderful surging joy of the Holy Spirit filling me. It flowed over me in waves of love and relief. I knew it was Jesus saying "He's OK". I jumped out of bed, knelt down and gave thanks for his healing. The following morning as the X-ray pictures of the dye flowing through the kidneys were taken, the doctor said "So far, so good". I was able to say "There's nothing wrong, there is no blockage." "How do you know?" "The Lord told me last night." The doctor just said "I hope you're right", and sure enough it was so. I praised God.

There are Healing Services in some of the major denominational Churches in Sydney as well as all the Charismatic or Pentecostal groups, which the sick may attend, or those who feel lead to pray for the sick. One of these services was held at Christ Church St. Lawrence, in those days led by Father John Hope.

My father was ill following a gall-bladder operation and couldn't leave hospital because the wound kept discharging. He was finally taken to X-ray, but the flow suddenly stopped at just the time he was being prayed for at Christ Church. Some time later his friend, a first-war digger was told he would probably lose his only leg. The other had been removed because of gangrene some years before. Now gangrene had set up in the foot. The situation looked hopeless, the surgeon called.

I wrote to him and said "I'll have the laying-on-of-hands on your behalf at 2pm tomorrow. Please try to be alone at this time, and in prayer, according to James 5:14,15:

'Is anyone among you sick? Let him call for the elders of the church and let them pray over him ..... and the prayer of faith will save the sick, and the Lord will raise him up. And if he has committed sins, he will be forgiven.'

I suggest you hand your life over to Jesus, and He will forgive your sins and heal you." When I was leaving the Church after the laying-on-of-hands, Belle my Aunt, was handing out notices at the door. Each had a notice of meeting times, a prayer and a verse. Belle had no idea what I was praying about, and handed me one of the cards at random. On it was the verse "I complained that I had no shoes until I met a man that had no feet."

Praise God, the healing was assured, this was a message to strengthen our faith. Within two or three weeks he was home, the only treatment for the previously gangrenous foot, lanoline.

My second daughter, Julia, was saved from what could have been a fatal accident. Playing on gymnastic bars in the back yard, she decided (age seven) to do a mid-air somersault as seen on TV. She had never attempted this before, but it looked so easy. I looked out the window in time to see Julia flying through the air, arms folded, straight onto her head. I instinctively cried "Jesus" and ran out. Julia was crying a high-pitched cerebral cry, blood-chilling really! Praise God, if her head had been tilted at all she would have broken her neck. She was carried inside and the doctor rung, but the only injury was a slight headache. What a wonderful God we have. We need to live really close to Him, to maintain a relationship with Jesus. The Bible says "The angel of the Lord encamps all around those who fear Him, and delivers them". Ps 34:7.

On the whole the Lord healed the family without

51

the intervention of the doctor, but very occasionally we called him. We must be careful we don't race to the phone every time someone is sick without asking the Lord "Why is this, is there something I can learn in this, are You saying something to me Lord? What is the lesson?" If we don't learn the lesson, often He brings us back to the same place again, and again, and again, round and round the mulberry bush until we catch on. On the other hand, sometimes we need medical attention. We musn't be foolish about this.

Once the Lord sent the doctor Himself. I was in the habit of eating with two friends after Scripture classes each Tuesday. I was on a weight-reducing diet, and only had one large honey-dew, while the others had sandwiches etc. This day I decided to eat the whole melon myself without offering to share. The melon was fermenting slightly, but still tasted good. The others said "That looks good". I said "Yes it is" and didn't offer any although I felt I should.

The following day there was poison coming out of nearly every pore of my head and my hands. My face was swollen like a "Monster from outer space", poison seeping out through the scalp, the line of the eyelashes, the pores of the nose, the ears and the fingers that had touched the melon. What a mess! I prayed and my morning reading was from Matthew 9:12 "Those who are well have no need of a physician, but those who are sick." I said "OK Lord, I'll ring the doctor after I run the children to school". Coming home I saw the doctor's car immediately behind me. I slowed till he passed and followed him to his sick call. "Doctor, I think I'm allergic to something". He said "Are you ever! I'll be round after this call", and put me onto Cortisone.

Praise God though, the lesson was learnt. We

mustn't be greedy but loving. Apart from a few minor instances like this, I reared the children trusting in the Lord for their healing. No bone was broken, and I seem to remember that Lindsay only had one day home sick all the years of Senior School.

I was healed from a Thyroxin dependence, trusting in the Lord. I'd tried a few times giving up the tablets, and each time suddenly collapsed. But the Lord has His perfect time. I was going away for a week's holiday, checked and rechecked to make sure I had my tablets, but when leaving took the wrong handbag. When I found that the tablets were back in Sydney, I prayed and said "Lord, this is really significant. Perhaps this is Your special time to heal me. I'll ask the Chemist for twenty one Thyroxin to last the week. If he says "No" I'll take it as from You." The Chemist refused point blank to give the tablets, which he said were on the dangerous drug list, so I left rejoicing, and never needed another tablet, completely healed.

I also received a healing at St. Andrews Cathedral, through Agnes Sanford. Through the shock of the plane crash, and the consequent break in marital relations, my periods stopped. At thirty five this is most undesirable. The doctors tried to heal with hormone treatment, but without success. Agnes Sanford was conducting a healing teaching mission, and on Monday night told everyone present to pray for a project, and she would pray that their prayers would be answered.

I had forgotten my problem, and prayed for my father's conversion, but the following day my periods came back, after eighteen months remission. They remained perfectly regular for the next fifteen years.

And so God provides Divine Health:

"If you diligently heed the voice of the Lord your God and do what is right in His sight, give ear to

His commandments and keep all His statutes, I will put none of the diseases on you which I have brought on the Egyptians. For I am the Lord Who heals you." Ex. 15:26.

"So you shall serve the Lord your God, and He will bless your bread and your water. And I will take sickness away from the midst of you". Ex. 23:25.

"And the Lord will take away from you all sickness". Deut. 7:14.

This I can verify. I've only had to call the doctor three times in the last thirty years myself, and no more than a dozen times in the nineteen years I was rearing the children. God is faithful.

## Getting to Know Him

When we find someone we love, we want to get to know all about that person. We long to be with them, talking or just sitting quietly holding hands. As the relationship deepens our heart is filled with love. Day and night we long to be with them.

To know Jesus in a personal relationship is a love that transcends all others. He wants us to know Him.

As Adam walked and talked with God in the garden, as Enoch "walked with God and was not, for God took him", Jesus wants us to walk and talk with Him.

I found the easiest way to walk and talk with Jesus was on my knees in the bedroom with the open Bible on the bed before me. As I prayed and talked with Him He often answered me from the Word. We had tremendous times together through the Holy Spirit opening up the Scriptures to me. Jesus was real.

Jesus had promised to be a Husband to me and a Father to my fatherless children. If I had a decision to make I just knelt, committed my dilemma to Him, waited before Him silently and then read the Word. He answered me almost every time.

One example of this occurred when I first became a Christian. I often tried to ring Christine to share with her. This was generally what the children had done or things I felt God was saying to me. Usually her number was either engaged, or she was out. "Why Lord? I need someone to share with." Then He gave me Song of Solomon 8:13.

"Your companions listen for your voice - let Me hear it".

"That's it Lord. You want us to share things with You most of all."

I made the discovery that to know Him is to love Him. We don't get to know people till we talk to them and share with them. Get to know Jesus personally.

My main object in life became the desire to cultivate a relationship with God. God the Son was the easiest to relate to because He came in a human body. He walked and talked with people who "beheld His glory, the glory as of the only-begotten of the Father, full of grace and truth." Getting to know Him through the Word, and the Holy Spirit, we are being conformed into His image. We are His betrothed, the Body of Christ, and we are to reach out to become like Him. "The Bride is making herself ready." We can only do this in the power of the Holy Spirit.

I was reaching out to know the Father too. One of the great joys of the Son is to bring us to the Father that we may Know Him. "No one comes to the Father except through Me." says Jesus.    John 14:6.

My main aim was to come into a relationship with God.

# Chapter 4
# Intercession

Now I was to learn a lesson about Intercession.

God taught the Israelites in the wilderness to pray and intercede when Amelek came against them to battle. In Ex 17:8 Moses stood on the top of the hill with Aaron and Hur, with the rod of God in his hand, and they found that when he lifted his hand in prayer Israel prevailed, and when he dropped his hand for weariness Amelek prevailed. Aaron and Hur held up his hands until sundown, and the victory was Israel's. Very early in their journey through the wilderness God taught His people to pray.

In order to pray properly for people we must love them, or have a heart of compassion for them. If we don't pray for those we love, who will?

I remember asking Christine what Intercession was. She told me "It is the most wonderful Christian gift. It is the Lord's own ministry. He sits on the right hand of the Father ever interceeding for us." I asked Him if he would give me the gift of Intercession.

God gives His great love to us to cause us to intercede. The children entered into much of my intercession. We prayed intercessory prayers while saying grace. Often this meant cold food in our house. The Lord sometimes laid on me the symptoms of those for whom I prayed.

We prayed for a well-known clergyman with cancer of the throat. He recovered and had a further fifteen years ministry.

Another on our intercessory list was a girl of fifteen who still wet the bed every night. Her mother was distraught about this, and the girl herself far too embarassed to speak about it. Her self-esteem was almost totally gone. She wouldn't sleep at anyone else's house and was becoming withdrawn and disturbed. It burdened my heart so much that one morning I was dismayed to find that I'd identified so much with her that I'd wet the bed myself (for the first and last time fortunately). She was healed.

Her brother had had rheumatic fever a few years before, and when he went into hospital for a tonsillectomy the surgeon was concerned about the anaesthetic. Vomiting might weaken his heart further, or even cause a heart attack. The day of the operation dawned with me vomiting, most unusual for me. I was sick about every half hour all through the day. Johnnie survived the operation wonderfully, no sign of vomiting at all. God was so good.

One of the most marvellous incidents happened in a very unusual type of intercession. One of my friends gave her heart to Jesus and was 'born again'. The next day she asked if I would speak to her husband Tom. Perhaps he would receive Jesus too. We prayed that this would happen at the right time. Tom asked me to visit them on Tuesday night.

I related the story of my own conversion, how Bob's plane crashed just past the "point of no return" (when there is not enough fuel to go back), but that through his death we found Jesus.

We talked of the circumstances of the flight, the rescue attempts.

At the appropriate time Jan went to the kitchen to make coffee, and I asked Tom if he would like to ask Jesus into his heart as Lord and Saviour. He prayed a prayer for forgiveness and acceptance, and the following morning sealed this by attending Communion.

In the afternoon he rang highly excited. "Have

you seen the evening papers?" On the front page was a map of the area we had been talking about the previous night, a dotted line from San Fransisco to Honolulu, and the story of an engine that cut out just past the point of no return. The headlines were "Crippled Plane lands in time - thirteen minutes left". (It arrived at Honolulu with thirteen minutes fuel left). Praise God, and if that wasn't enough, another plane the following night was saved on the same route, 90 odd aboard. Lord, You're wonderful. Tom was greatly encouraged. God used this preaching of the Gospel in intercession.

And there's more! I was asked to speak about eighteen months later at a Women's group at Northbridge. I prayed that the date would be right, and it turned out to be the seventh anniversary of Bob's death, ninth November, '64. Again I told the story of finding Jesus through the crash and offered an invitation to anyone who wasn't born again. The next day, a Pan Am jet dropped 11,500ft on the Los Angeles/ Honolulu route. No-one hurt. God is supreme:

"As the heavens are higher than the earth, so are My ways higher than your ways, and My thoughts than your thoughts." Is 55:9.

There was a photograph in a magazine which troubled me - a row of coffins (deaths in some African massacre). I'd opened the magazine right at this page. Not understanding what was happening I prayed "God, I don't understand this, but I know You are speaking to my spirit. Please save those who are in danger." That weekend there was a fire at SCEGGS Moss Vale in the girl's dormitory. Praise God no-one was hurt.

Some years later I also accidently turned up this picture, failed to pray, and overnight some elderly men were burnt to death in a hostel fire in Sydney.

The ministry of Intercession carries with it great responsibility. I feel that if I had interceeded at this time those men would have been rescued. Forgive me Lord. Once having asked the Lord for forgiveness and cleansing, by faith we receive it, and must not allow ourselves to come into self-condemnation. Condemnation is one of the devil's greatest weapons.

## Intercession for the Jews

I began to realise that Intercession is a ministry that is available to any Christian who asks for it, but particularly for those "with time". I am reminded of the little boy who was asked to write a description of a Grandmother. He began by saying "Grandmas have time."

People "Shut in" by sickness, infirmity, old age, mothers with babies and young children are amongst the people "with time". It is a great asset in intercession.

Being a "shut-in" Mum until Margie was school age, I had a great opportunity for prayer and intercession, and I loved every moment alone with the Lord.

I heard through a missionary talk that God has a plan for His people, the Jews, and my heart stirred within me. "My God, if ever I became a missionary I would want above all to be a missionary to Your own people. What a privilege to be called to witness to the Jews, above all people on the face of the earth."

In the future the Lord would take me up on this!

There was a young minister named Deane who had been called by God to witness to the Falashas, a tribe of Jews in Ethiopia. The Falasha tribe claims to be descended from a union between the Queen of Sheba and Solomon and/or fugitives from the tribe of Dan after the Babylonian dispersion. Deane was learning Hebrew, but had been unable to obtain an Ethiopian visa. I met Deane and his fiancee and promised to pray for them.

I asked the Lord "How would You have me pray?" He showed me Jeremiah 22:10:

"Weep not for the dead, nor bemoan him, but weep bitterly for him who goes away, for he shall return no more nor see his native country."

The Holy Spirit was saying to me "Don't weep for Bob, he is dead and will not return, but weep bitterly for Deane because he will die abroad on the mission field."

I was so shocked! I loved Deane and believed in his calling. Deane's life Jesus laid heavily on my heart. I prayed and I prayed and I prayed. This intercession remained for some years.

There was no-one I could share this secret with. Paul and Christine were his close friends and might let something slip. It is not wise to let some people know you are praying for them so deeply. It puts them under a sort of obligation or even a feeling of being dominated or controlled. This drove me closer to the Lord in prayer and petition.

At last I felt I must share this with another person. I rang a dear man, Mr. Perrett, much wiser and older than I, a Christian of long standing. He was also of another denomination and would probably not know Deane. He agreed to come and talk with me after dinner.

Before he came I prayed and opened the scriptures straight at Proverbs 3:26:

"For the Lord will be your confidence, and will keep your foot from being caught." (Confidence here meant 'confiding', my foot would be caught if I broke His confidence.)

v27 Do not withhold good from those to whom it is due, when it is in the power of your hand to do so. (My prayer will work.)

v28 Do not say to your neighbour 'Go, and come back, and tomorrow I will give it' when you have it with you. (Pray now.)

v29 Do not devise evil against your neighbour, for he dwells by you for safety's sake, (thinking 'I don't want this responsibility, wish I'd never set eyes on him, but he dwells securely by my prayer')

v30 Do not strive with a man without cause, if he has done you no harm (don't write him off just because you feel burdened).

v31 Do not envy the oppressor and choose none of his ways;

v32 For the perverse person is an abomination to the Lord, but His secret is with the upright". (Yes Lord, thankyou for this secret, I will keep it and play my part.)

I rang Mr. Perrett and told him not to come.

And so the story has never been told, until today.

The intercession continued. I repeatedly received verses like Ps 79:11 "Let the groaning of the prisoner come before You, according to the greatness of Your power preserve those who are appointed to die."

I prayed. All day and much of the night, I prayed.

Paul, one of the leaders of this particular missionary society suspected that I had a secret, and said "I often find that a special prayer burden is given to one person before a missionary leaves, and I try to find out who that person is." I had been told by the Lord to keep my knowledge to myself, so I just looked at him blankly, what else could I do?

Deane and his fiancée Elizabeth were married and attended a missionary convention before leaving for the mission field. They had found it impossible to enter Ethiopia as the visas could not be obtained, so were transferring to Tanzania.

I had originally been praying for the Jews, but now Deane's welfare had been laid on me. "God I just can't handle this, don't ask me to speak to him or share any of this, I can't cope, and I won't speak." God gave me a verse in Psalm 32:8,9:

"I will instruct you and teach you in the way you should go; I will guide you with My eye. Do not be like the horse or the mule, which have no understanding, which must be harnessed with bit and bridle...." In other words, "Don't get the bit in your teeth and race off ahead of Me, and don't sit down like the mule and refuse to budge. I will instruct and teach you."

Deane was one of the speakers at the Convention. I really didn't know what to expect next. In order to have an uninterrupted Quiet Time with God I drove to Echo Point and laid my Bible open on the park bench. There was absolutely no wind, but suddenly the pages turned over and then smoothed out in an awesome way.

The Holy Spirit showed me He had a message. I was standing a few feet from the Bible, walked to it and the message just jumped out from Isaiah 56:1:

"Thus says the Lord: 'Keep justice, and do righteousness, for My salvation is about to come, and My righteousness to be revealed."

Thankyou Lord, please strengthen me and help me know Your will.

I spent every afternoon that week in Church praying, worshipping and reading the Bible. One afternoon I suddenly felt the presence of God. My eyes fell on the open Bible at Isaiah 41:1:

"Keep silence before Me....."

I fell to my knees. Words of comfort flowed from Is. 41-44, with many "Fear nots". Suddenly he gave me a touch of His power.

I felt as though I was surrounded by dozens of vibrating Power Stations (this is the only way I can describe the power). Tremendous power! My body twisted from side to side with the great current and pressure, and I called out "Lord stop, I'll die". Ever since that time I've wished I hadn't asked Him to stop, He wouldn't have allowed me to die, but I was frightened and completely awestruck.

That night Deane preached. Suddenly under the power of the Spirit he turned to me and spoke in prophecy "If you will only forget yourself, there will be revival in the Falasha Tribe." As he said this the Holy Spirit came on me again and I began jerking with the power as I had done in St. Hilda's that afternoon. Deane told Paul later that he had never seen anything like that before in his life.

Years later someone spoke to me about the night the Holy Spirit came down upon the meeting at Katoomba. This was the occasion. On the last day of the Convention I was in the Church praying, and opened my Bible quickly in two places looking for a certain verse, but the two messages the Lord gave me were from Jeremiah 33:3:

"Call unto Me and I will answer you and show you great and mighty things which you do not know",

and Jeremiah 22:10:

"Weep bitterly for him who goes away....for he shall return no more...."

Thankyou Lord, You will show me more about praying for Deane.

During the evening Deane's secretary Marie came to speak to me and said "I'm pleased he and his wife are not going to Ethiopia, because I had a terrible dream. He was trying to dig through the walls to get into the land, and the Ethiopians ran at him with axes and chopped his head off. There was blood everywhere, it was so vivid I was nearly sick."

My God! I was stunned! Words failed me. So this is what the Lord was wanting to tell me!

This was verified to me in a talk by Bishop Wiggins, on leave from Tanzania, speaking to a Bible study group in my own lounge room, about Africa and the Literacy Programme. He said "The alphabet is shown in picture form. For example the letter 'D' is shown as a man with an axe in his hand, held above his head and brought down in a full sweep to form 'D' for Dumela, to behead.

God also revealed to me that the twisting of Deane's neck (or 'tic') was a physical sign of the beheading which was to befall him unless I interceeded. 1 Sam. 12:23:

> "Far be it from me that I should sin against the Lord in ceasing to pray for you; but I will teach you the good and the right way."

Reports came through about atrocities in Portuguese East Africa (March '61), many whites and Africans chopped up by machettes, often horribly wounded. One young girl was chopped in half.

Then we heard of an army near Deane's mission quarters. "Keep the family safe Lord." And so the prayers kept ascending. This type of intercession is truly of the Holy Spirit, one is locked into it, and there is no escape. And it must be done in Agape Love - no response necessary from the person concerned. Deane was totally oblivious of the situation, and still is.

Agape (God's kind of love) loves regardless. It never ends, unless the Holy Spirit lifts the load, which happened when he returned home. At that time I asked "How did things go in Africa?" and he replied that at one time there was a disturbance near his village. He went down to see what the matter was and found some of the trouble-makers armed with axes. "I thought there might be bloodshed - perhaps even mine" he said.

Thankyou Lord for intercession, and his safe "return to his native country".

# Chapter 5
# Teaching

Paul realised I was a person who loved to study and learn, so he helped me enter a three year diploma course through Moore College (IVFC), and later the RITC (Religious Instruction Teacher's Certificate) through the Anglican Board of Education.

Verification of my calling to teach Scripture came the very term Margie turned five, and began school. I knew that I could get a Scripture class anywhere, Scripture teachers are always very scarce. I asked the Lord to bring the ministers to me rather than contacting them myself, and in this way I would know that they were the classes given to me by Him.

The local curate, who didn't know I was waiting for a word from the Lord, nor that I was now free to teach, knocked at the door asking if I'd take a third class at Lindfield school. He stopped for a cup of coffee and I showed him some commentaries formerly owned by Archbishop Mowell. In one of these was written some words in Greek, which the curate translated "Feed My lambs". Just the very words to stir me to teach. Thankyou Lord.

And so began thirteen years of Scripture teaching in the State schools. My ten classes a week ranged from sub-normal children to sixth year boys.

I was amused how the teachers sorted out the migrant children in the infants school. Many of the children couldn't speak English, having just arrived in Australia, and many other littlies didn't know what their religion was. If there was any doubt, the ones with gold earrings were put into the Catholic group and most of the others were called Anglican (unless there were special instructions from the parents). These migrant children spilled into my ever-expanding Anglican class.

The primary children were precious. One little boy asked, "Is God Presbyterian or Catholic or Baptist?" Another child said, when told that there will be no sorrow or tears or sickness in Heaven "Oh, I know there won't be any crying in Heaven, we'll all be dead."

The Lord has wonderful ways of teaching us. At a well-known Sydney Girls High School I had a very unruly third year girls' class. Vicki, one of the girls aged about fifteen deliberately set out to wreck each Scripture lesson. She was repeatedly sent to the Headmistress, but was defiant and rude each week. On one particular occasion she was so badly behaved I got angry, and really began exhuding hate and frustration towards her.

Exhausted by my confrontation with Vicki, I prayed about the situation after arriving home. The Lord gave me an example from Elisha's life in 2 Kings 2:23, 24 about the children calling him "You bald head":

"And as he was going up the road, some youths came from the city and mocked him, and said to him 'Go up, you baldhead! Go up you baldhead!' So he turned around and looked at them, and pronounced a curse on them in the name of the Lord. And two female bears came out of the woods and mauled forty-two of the youths."

The Lord was saying "Be careful you don't curse this troublesome girl. Elisha was a man of God who forgot what authority he had in the Lord's name. A Christian has great power for good, but also great power for evil. If you lose your temper with Vicki you may bring hurt upon her."

I repented of my dislike and then God gave me Matt. 5:11,12:

"Blessed are you when they revile and persecute you, and say all kinds of evil against you falsely for My sake. Rejoice and be exceedingly glad for great is your reward in Heaven, for so they persecuted the prophets who were before you."

"Thank God. I'm getting a reward, I'm going to Heaven, He's likening me to the prophets". This made my day. What wonderful ways the Lord uses to encourage us.

Years later I was at a Children's Seminar and the Lord spoke to me in the Spirit saying "I am healing you from hurts you received as a Scripture Teacher." I hadn't realised how deeply some of these experiences had affected me.

It is so important to reach children while they are young. "Train up a child in the way he should go, and when he is old he will not depart from it." Prov 22:6. As the twig is bent, so is the tree inclined. Children should be brought up in the "fear and nurture of the Lord." If they were, there would be fewer rebellious young people. In the Old Testament laws given to Moses, a rebellious son was to be stoned to death. This is what God thinks about rebellion. He loves the sinner, but hates the sin. Lucifer was rebellious, as were Adam and Eve. What sorrow rebellion brings into our world.

# Chapter 6
# Faith Builders

God taught me His principles in many different ways; the following examples show some of the practical ways in which He did it.

## a) The Spoken Word

A Psoralia bush growing in the back garden was looking straggly, and I spoke to it as I walked past. "You are an ugly bush, one of these days I'll have you chopped down." That night there was a fierce storm, lots of wind, and in the morning the Psoralia was lying flat on the ground, split in halves. Nothing else in the garden was harmed.

We often don't realise the power of our negative pronouncements, or our positive words of faith. Our words can shape our lives. What you say is indeed what you get. "I'm pleased I didn't really hate Vicki", I thought.

## b) Trip to Kiama

As a special treat I wanted to take the family on a Steam Train journey before the old "Puff-puffs" were gone. There was only one steam train out of Sydney - the South Coast Mail.

The family prayed for the right day, and bought return tickets to Kiama, a day trip. We had hoped for a windy day, because the Blow Hole only blows high with reasonably heavy seas, but the day was sunny and calm. However, God is so good and probably smiled a little. Arriving at Kiama we found the blowhole was blowing so high (about 50 feet) that the people were getting wet in the spray. There had been earthquakes in Chile a few days before, affecting the ocean floor. Big waves, travelling across the Pacific, arrived that day. It's an ill wind that blows no good, and even praying about the right day to go on a picnic is not too trivial for our God.

## c) Gold Stole

I had a special invitation to dinner and the Theatre, and wanted to look exceptionally smart. All my best jewellery was silver, but my favourite stole was heavily woven with gold. In those days it simply wasn't done to wear gold and silver together, so I prayed about it. "Lord, please help me to look just right". The Lord gave me assurance from Psalm 68:13:

"You will be like the wings of a dove covered with silver, and her feathers with yellow gold".

The Lord is interested in the most intimate details of our lives. If He knows when a sparrow falls to the ground, and is concerned enough to refer to it, if the hairs of our head are all numbered, we needn't think anything is unimportant. My Mother-in-law once said "My dear, God is far too busy to be interested in something small like that." Fortunately for us, this is not so.

## May I Go Lord?

I wanted to attend a Conference, but always prayed for permission when making arrangements for a holiday, as there were five persons concerned, four children and myself. I really needed the Lord's assurance that the plans were OK. He answered from Jeremiah 49:11:

> "Leave your fatherless children, I will preserve them alive; and let your widows trust in Me."

The children were either able to go to Christian Camps or their Grandmother.

On another occasion I wanted to attend a yearly convention. Every year He gave me permission to go. This year, however, was different. The answer was "No".

"Please Lord, please let me go." "No." "Please Lord, You know how much I depend on those meetings for spiritual strength." "All right, go." I was overjoyed, but reading the Bible that night I was up to the story of Balaam. Balaam wanted to go on a journey, God said "No". Balaam pleaded and finally the Lord said "All right, go", but the whole venture was a disaster. This was enough for me. "Thankyou Lord, You know best."

The Convention was disappointing by all accounts. It rained heavily every day and some cars were bogged. God opened up something far better the following week to which the children were invited as well.

No wonder Martin Luther said "Kill reason and trust God."

Then He showed me another facet of His love.

# Beryl

One of my dear friends was dying of cancer. Only young, she had a loving husband and two beautiful sons, one of whom had just completed the Higher school Certificate exams.

Hearing about my conversion and eternal life and forgiveness in Jesus, she handed her life over to Him. She sent a message before she died "Tell Ruth what she said to me was not wasted." Before she died the news of her son's good pass in the HSC was given her, and she passed away an hour later. At the funeral the Minister said "She had a new-found faith, and said 'I am ready to go'!"

Praise God, it's only through Jesus we can be sure that we will live forever in Heaven.    1 John 5:12:

"He who has the Son has life; he who does not have the Son of God does not have life."

# Chapter 7
# Growing As Christians

## a) Giving

The Lord now began to teach me the laws of prosperity. A believer who really desires to walk by faith should be giving to God one tenth of his gross income, plus offerings. Mal. 3:8-12. I was unaware of this, nevertheless had given to various Christian needs. I had an amount of money for re-investment, prayed about it and the Lord showed me to give it to a needy Christian cause. Then another amount fell due for re-investment. I panicked "Lord, if I keep giving money every time it's due for re-investment I'll finish up with nothing. And how do I know that it's not the devil telling me to do it to bring us to poverty."

The Lord said "Pray about it." "No." "Pray about it". "No, I don't want to give it". "Pray about it". This went on for some days till finally I slammed my finger in the car door, and the nail went black. After this I gave in, and said "Lord, I am willing. Where do You want me to give this money?" "I don't want it at this time, I just wanted your obedience."

I had a black fingernail for about three months until the nail grew. I felt like David who said in Psalm 51:3 "My sin is ever before me." Every day, as I caught sight of it through the day, the black nail lesson hit home.

There was another large gift to be given, but the Lord spoke through a hymn:

"Ye fearful saints, fresh courage take,
the clouds ye so much dread

Are big with mercy and will break
In blessings on your head."

These gifts I was so reluctant to give changed my whole life in a wonderful way. They "opened up the windows of heaven" and the Lord poured out His blessings on my life. My relationship with Jesus deepened. I believe the obedience to His command to give specifically to this missionary call has enabled God to bring me to a new spiritual depth. This includes His wonderful care of my children and their spiritual growth.

# b) Sunday School and Church

The children used to laugh and say that if nothing else, they always got the prize for good attendance at Sunday School. Rain hail and shine we were in Sunday School and Church on Sundays. The Lord was our strength, our life blood.

Unbeknown to me, James had been warned about his behaviour in Sunday School and the Superintendant had threatened to tell his mother. James got in first, however, and asked me if he could join the Choir. Sunday School and Church were conducted at the same time, so I was delighted. What a dedicated good little boy he was. By the time I found out about the behaviour problems he was well ensconced in the Choir. James looked so angelic in his robes. It wasn't all easy for him though. Being in the Choir he was under the eagle eye of his mother. Praise God, all things work together for good!

The Church Camps the children looked forward to attending every school vacation were amongst our greatest blessings. They learnt canoeing, water safety, cooking, rock-climbing, absailing etc., also leadership, as well as knowing God.

## c) Birthday Parties

Compared with most other mothers I was apparently considered "strange" and "religious". The children tease me now about their birthday parties. Theirs were the only parties where an invitation to receive Jesus was given before cutting the cake. When James was about eight or nine, at his party I took fifteen of his schoolmates to see "The Greatest Story Ever Told", with the aid of one of the fathers.

The Lord even taught us a few lessons through the cats. Someone smacked the kitten, and she immediately got a bone caught in her throat. Once I lost my temper with the cat, chased it outside. It was scratched right across the eye in a cat fight shortly after. If we give place to anger, it opens the way to evil. God's kingdom runs on love. Violate the laws of love in any way, and you will reap what you have sown. Sow to the wind, and you'll reap the whirlwind.

# Chapter 8
# Incidents Along The Way

## a) Daddy's Death

I'd never enjoyed a close relationship with my Father and because of this bad start had become very rebellious towards him. Although he obviously loved me, we didn't have a close cuddling relationship. However over the last few years the relationship had improved tremendously, and we did have some good times sharing together. He listened somewhat impatiently when I spoke to him of spiritual things, and changed the subject as soon as possible. Aren't families just the most difficult people to witness to!

When the '59 Graham Crusade was on in Sydney I took him one night, and was disappointed that he didn't go forward for Christ. He assured me afterwards that he had given his heart to Jesus at about eighteen or nineteen years of age when he played the Organ in a Baptist Church, and attended a Methodist Bible Study.

As far as I was concerned, this was one of the best-kept secrets of the century. Why don't Christian parents share these commitments with their children? What a difference it would have made in our lives! When I asked what he wanted for his birthday he said he'd like a New English New Testament (just published). He loved it.

Then unfortuantley he found out that I had given some money to a Christian Mission (a considerable amount), and he was so offended he put the Bible in a cupboard and didn't open it again. He also disinherited me, and once more our relationship was strained. "Lord, I believe You asked me to give that money, and now look what's happened! Daddy said I was out of my mind, and would not discuss Christian things at all, they were taboo!"

Some years later we found he had cancer in the lung, in a very advanced form apparently, because he was dead in four weeks.

I visited him in hospital every day for the two weeks he was there, and said "Daddy, I'd like to read to you from John if I may, perhaps a chapter a day?" He agreed, and seemed to cherish the readings. After two weeks he badly wanted to go home, so the doctor, who said there was nothing more to be done for him, sent him home to die.

Two weeks later I had a ring from my Aunt "Have a bite of lunch, and then come up to see your Father, I don't think he will last the day."

I went into my bedroom, knelt and prayed and took the Bible. It opened at Job 14 and I knew the Lord was telling me he would die. This passage is generally read at funerals. Job 14:

> v1 "Man who is born of woman is of few days and full of trouble.
>
> v2 He comes forth like a flower and fades away; he flees like a shadow and does not continue.
>
> v4 Who can bring a clean thing out of an unclean?
>
> v5 Since his days are determined, the number of his months is with You, You have appointed his limits, so that he cannot pass.
>
> v10 But man dies and is laid away; indeed he breathes his last and where is he?
>
> v12 So man lies down and does not rise.
>
> v14 If a man dies, shall he live again?
>
> v20 You change his countenance and send him away."

When I arrived daddy was propped up in bed, breathing very laboriously. He opened his eyes momentarily and smiled. I took his hand in mine and sat with him for a couple of hours.

He was not to be told he was dying, at my mother's request. Every fifteen minutes or so I would just squeeze his hand and say "Think of Jesus, daddy", and he would squeeze back. After a time I realised with a sinking heart that his hand was beginning to grow cold, from his fingers. Finally when I squeezed, he didn't respond. He was now unconscious.

As death approached, my mother, aunt and I sat round the bed, with a nurse in attendance. Daddy's breathing became irregular, sometimes missing a breath altogether, and then, just when we thought he'd gone, he would start breathing again. Each time he missed a breath my spirit would rise within me and I'd say "Here he comes Jesus", "Here he comes". I felt joyful and excited as I thought of his spirit coming out of the body to be with Jesus. Only God can transform tragic death into great peace and triumph.

As he breathed for the last time, and the spirit left, I called out silently "Here he is Lord,' and felt quite envious. My daddy was now seeing Jesus face to face. Glory to God. One of the others said "He's gone", but I was rejoicing "He's arrived!"

"Who can bring a clean thing out of an unclean?" God can, Jesus can, His cleansed spirit leaving the unclean body. Later I went to his room to say goodbye. He looked waxen and altogether different, and I remembered the verse from Job that Jesus had shown me some hours before, "You change his countenance and send him away."

Thankyou God, You are so kind. I know Daddy is born again, and with You. Before he died he said to me "When I go, will you look after mummy for me?"

and I promised I would. She too became a Christian in a most miraculous way, which I'll write about later. She and my father are together with the Lord. "Great is Your faithfulness O God my Father." I risked my daddy's disapproval when You asked me for an offering, but You more than made it up to me at his death.

## b) Joe

A breath of fresh air suddenly blew into the lives of the Halliday family in the person of Joe.

Joe and Randy were Julia's friends. They sometimes drove her home from school and called in for coffee. Joe's parents worked in the evening, and he didn't like the empty house or the loneliness of eating alone, so he joined us for meals. He began calling me "Mum" and our place "Home', and we loved him as one of the family.

Joe didn't realise how he was helping me, but I had very nearly become entangled in a disastrous relationship with a would-be lover, and Joe's constant presence in the home helped keep the other person at a distance, because they knew one another. In fact, Joe was the direct provision of the Lord. David and Bathsheba warnings were coming over to me loud and clear in sermons, books etc. I prayed "Lord help me, I don't want to become involved with this married man but I'm feeling so lonely and so weak".

The Lord gave me Judges 3:15:

"When the children of Israel cried out to the Lord, the Lord raised up a deliverer for them: Ehud .... a left-handed man."

Praise God, Joe was my deliverer, a left-handed man.

Joe was such a needy soul in many ways, but a terror behind the wheel of a car, wheelies around corners, laying rubber etc. A screech of brakes during the night, and we would say "That's Joe!"

And then the Lord laid an intercession on me. He gave the scripture Job 34:25:

"He overturns them in the night and they are crushed."

My God, save him! I carried this burden for months. Joe's current second hand car was an open tourer, with no hood.

Then came the night when he and I had a heated argument, and he stamped out the back door, into the car, gravel scattering as he pressed the accelerator to the floor in reverse. With a screeching of tyres, away he went. Randy and Julia were with him, and I was at home exhuding hate and wondering why on earth I ever put up with such appalling behaviour.

Ten minutes later there was a knock at the back door. When I opened the door there stood Randy and Julia, torn clothes, gravel rashes, cuts, blood, dirt. Julia just said "Mum, we fell out of the car." Joe had driven screeching around a corner and skidded in the gravel. Randy and Julia were thrown against the door, which burst open, and out they rolled.

I patched them up, bathed their wounds. Joe was quite distraught. Praise God the car didn't roll, or they would all have been killed. Perhaps the intercession was largely about this incident.

Then the Lord gave a test of patience, but a wonderful blessing in the end. The family was attending a Convention of Katoomba, and Joe decided to drive up for the evening meeting. He arrived at midnight quite distressed and said his car (a second-hand bomb) had broken down, could I get up and tow him to a garage? He said the car was on the Bell Road, which is twenty miles or more from Katoomba. I thought he must be mistaken, it couldn't possibly be on the Bell Road which was miles out of his way. We set out in heavy fog to tow the car.

The fog grew thicker as we drove up the mountains. At Blackheath the visibility was almost nil, too dangerous to turn the car around and go back, as heavy transporters were suddenly appearing out of the fog. We turned as soon as possible, and returned to the cottage. The next day we found the car, miles away on the Bell Road as he said. We attached the rope and towed up and down hills into Lithgow. Joe told me later that he kept the brakes on all the way in case he couldn't stop the car. Thanks Joe! When we reached the garage he had no money, so I paid the account.

The following day, reading my Bible, I was up to the parable of the Good Samaritan. Luke 10: 29-37 Living Bible:

"But a Samaritan, when he saw him, felt deep pity. Kneeling beside him the Samaritan soothed his wounds with medicine and bandaged them. Then he put the man on his donkey and walked along beside him" (towed Joe's car slowly) "till they came to an inn' (a garage) "where he nursed him through the night" (where the car stayed overnight for repairs). "The next day he handed the innkeeper two twenty dollar bills" (the repairs cost forty dollars, which I had paid with two twenty dollar bills). "If the bill runs higher than that, he said, I'll pay the difference." (I had said 'I'll lend you the money if you need any more repairs to the car').

Amazing. Thankyou Lord, You are so encouraging.

The intercession re overturning the car was still heavy on me, but thank God Joe was now driving a Fiat Sedan. He went for a holiday and while he was away rolled the car. It skidded about thirty feet on its roof, five young people inside. One had his arm out the window, and suffered injury, but praise God, without the prayer it could have been much worse, all killed perhaps.

Joe said "You looking after me has changed the whole of my life". Shortly afterwards he took up a new life style, and we rarely saw him.

"Joe, if you read this book, we love you, and wouldn't have missed the experiences together for anything. We thank God for having known you."

## c) Peter Rabbit

Margie had a beautiful white Angora rabbit called "Peter". He had long floppy ears which were pink inside, pink eyes, a snuffly pink nose and strong back feet with which he would thump.

Margie used to pretend to scold him when he hopped over to the crab-apple tree and ate the apples lying on the ground. "Peter, what are you doing eating those apples? We want them for crab-apple jelly." But Peter would look at her and thump, and go on eating.

Peter had a male friend called "the Black Rabbit" or "Blackie", and they both lived in a burrow in the back yard under a gum tree, which had a wire aviary enclosure around it. It was useless trying to keep them in the cage, because at night they would burrow out. If we stopped up the burrow they just dug another one. I was too soft-hearted to put wire under their feet.

Peter and Blackie used to run on the tennis court and leap in the air stretching their back legs at dusk, and often hop down the footpath together, calling in to neighbour's gardens to eat a few flowers etc. The neighbours loved them.

Then a new family arrived across the street. The man had a gun. He shot a few magpies, and some people called to complain. He said "Well, what else can I shoot?"

Early one morning I heard the crack of a rifle and went out to investigate. I found Peter's little white body lying on the man's back lawn. He complained that Peter was digging under his house undermining its foundations. He pointed out that the rabbit was on his property and he had every right to shoot it. I accused him of discharging a rifle in a built-up area, and reported the matter to the Police. They confiscated his gun.

Margie was heartbroken, the whole house upset, the neighbours angry.

After the children left for school I collapsed on the bed crying my heart out, the loneliness and responsibility of widowhood and single parenthood suddenly coming upon me in great waves of despair. I cried for a long time then sobbed "Lord Jesus, I have no-one but You to hold me, please comfort me Lord." I then thought "How does He generally speak to me? Through the Bible. To be comforted I must read that," so rolled off the bed onto my knee, wiped away the tears so that I could see the print and said "Lord, unless I rise from my knees smiling I'll feel You haven't comforted me." (No doubt a prayer from the Holy Spirit, because He knew what He would do).

The Holy Spirit had been calling me "Esther" for a few weeks, and the Bible fell open at Esther 2:17. I wiped my eyes again in order to read, and He showed me "The King loved Esther more than all the women, and she obtained grace and favour in his sight more than all the virgins; so he set the royal crown upon her head, and made her queen."

The Holy Spirit spoke this directly to my heart,

and I was filled with the comfort and joy and peace of the Lord. As I rose from my knees He reminded me "Hey, you're smiling!" I smile even now as I remember.

The Holy Spirit is the great Comforter.

As time passed I was looking for something new, something challenging to do as well as teaching.

Lindsay, my eldest daughter, suggested I join Lifeline Telephone Counselling Service, and be trained as a Counsellor. I applied to do the Course and was accepted, counselling with them for three years.

Seeing how overworked the Psychologist was I decided to go back to University, major in Psychology and help him on a voluntary basis. I commenced study at Macquarie University in the Faculty of Behavioural Sciences, and passed first year Psychology, Philosophy and Anthropology. I found with the pressure of assignments, lectures, running a home, Scripture teaching, rearing a family etc. that my spiritual life began to wane.

With this came a drop of spiritual standards. I was growing in knowledge and worldly wisdom, but my walk with the Lord began to slow down.

I had said years previously to the Lord "I'm not going out looking for a Christian husband because I might make a mistake. I want one Lord, the right one, and I'm waiting till You bring him to me."

And so I waited, and waited. Twelve years after Bob's death I was still waiting. No husband. "Lord, I'm getting a bit fed up with this." Then an unexpected turn of events. A significant man came into my life. He was attractive, intelligent, personable, exciting, loving ..... and married!

# Chapter 9
# Rebellion/Weariness/
# Depression

## a) Yohan

At last a kindred soul. Yohan and I were instantly attracted to one another, and a deep love relationship developed. We were both swept along by our great need, and our compatibility. The fact that his wife had left him some years previously didn't alter the fact that he was still a married man.

I had been reading a book called "The Strong and the Weak" by Paul Tournier, and decided to use some of the techniques explained therein to help heal some of his many hurts. The more I listened and listened to his deep needs, the more involved I became. I was beginning to learn the rudiments of counselling, and some of the traps! I was also practicing some of the Psychology I was learning at Uni. Gradually the relationship began to cut into our spiritual lives with the Lord. Many times we agreed to stop seeing one another, but after some weeks always finished up in one another's arms again, completely bound.

## Depression

My health deteriorated, as I was by this time quite out of fellowship with the Lord. Depression set in. Finally one day I said "I don't want to live any more", and then realised the depths to which I had sunk. Yohan was shocked, and suggested a visit to the doctor, who put me on anti-depressant medication. But the guilt, anxiety, worry, fear of being found out, despair, were taking their toll. I realised that Jesus was more to me than anything, and longed to get back into a close relationship with my Lord.

Bound tightly with the cords of physical fulfilment, I was powerless to break the ties.

Yohan spoke of divorce, but his wife, a Catholic, didn't believe in divorce, nor for that matter did I. "You can't build happiness on someone else's unhappiness" I told him. We sought an answer from the Lord.

I went to a meeting where the speaker talked about leprosy. In the Old Testament if there was any doubt about a sore, the Israelite showed it to the priest. If he was unsure, the man was shut up for one week and then the priest looked at the sore again. If still unsure, another week's confinement, and if the priest was still unsure, it was to be "treated as a leprosy'. God showed me through the teaching that this relationship was to be treated as a leprosy (or sin).

We found it almost impossible to part. We would decide "This is it! This is final! We won't see one another again." "Do you mind if I ring occasionally?" "Not often". "I must know how you are". "OK".

What wonderful goodbyes we had - tender kisses, tears, love-letters and then the inevitable phone call "I can't live without you any longer. May I come and see you just once more?"

And so it went on.

In desperation we prayed "Lord, there must be more power in the Christian life than this. Lord, we're so powerless. Lord help us, weak as we are."

The way the Lord gave us power was to fill us both with the Holy Spirit. Praise God. This is how it happened.

# b) Healing of Depression

I had been taking anti-depressants for a year now, and the doctor said he could do no more to heal me. I pointed out that what I really needed was a 'spiritual healing'. The doctor agreed "That would be helpful", but looked a little apprehensive.

I'd heard of healing in the Charismatic movement, and went along with a friend, Thelma, to the Holy Spirit seminar at the Hordern Pavilion. I had run out of anti-depressant tablets that morning, and hoped that this was a sign that I would be healed. As we entered the Pavilion the joyful strains of one of the praise choruses rose up "This is the day, this is the day that the Lord made, we will rejoice and be glad in it."

"That's what I need - Joy! To be able to rejoice!"

As the meeting progressed there were scriptures used that had been given me for healing before. My faith level rose.

The congregation began singing and praising and worshipping the Lord in tongues. "I've never heard anything so beautiful, how exciting to be able to praise the Lord in a new language". I was overwhelmed with the beauty of the worship. The sound of spiritual praises was like the surging of waters or a strong breeze through the treetops.

Thelma went forward for the laying-on-of-hands, but I was wary, and remained in my seat. Thelma said later "As they laid hands on my head all I could think of was you. I wanted you to come off your tablets and be healed of your depression."

All this time I was calling out "Lord, forgive my backsliding, Lord forgive me, forgive me, forgive me." Tears were streaming down my face. As hands were laid on Thelma, the Holy Spirit fell in power on me. Into my aching heart flooded the warmth and joy of the Holy Spirit. My heart had felt like a block of stone within me, but suddenly it began melting and I experienced what was promised in Ezek 36:26:

"I will give you a new heart and put a new spirit within you; I will take the heart of stone out of your flesh and give you a heart of flesh".

I knew I was healed.

Arriving home I said "Lord, I'm afraid to give up my tablets unless You give me a word". I walked over to a chorus sheet lying on the bench. My eyes fell on the last two lines "I only touched the hem of His garment, but His blood has made me whole."

I wrote to my doctor "I believe I have I have received the healing I spoke about. If I'm wrong I'll be back for more tablets, but if right I'll come and tell you anyway."

Three months later I returned and pointed out to the doctor that Jesus had healed me. A few weeks after this initial healing from the physical effects of depression, I again became depressed. I knew I didn't need any more tablets, and was puzzled. Thelma suggested I go the Epping Apostolic Church which she and her sister attended. One of the men had been filled with a spirit of joy after the Sunday meeting, and he and another young man started laughing and couldn't stop. "Let's go and find out about this."

We attended their prayer meeting on the Thursday evening, and when we entered the room those already gathered said "How are you girls?" "Depressed", said Thelma. "We'll soon fix that" was the reply.

The meeting began with stereotyped prayers, but later I opened my eyes to see two men standing, one on either side of me. "We're just going to lay our hands on your head and tell the spirit of depression to leave." "Great" I thought. They prayed simply, "spirit of depression, I command you to leave in

Jesus' name. Get out now." They prayed quietly in the Spirit for a short while, and then repeated the same prayers for Thelma. Neither of us felt any different.

The men resumed their seats, and then one of them began to laugh. He laughed and laughed, and his friend across the room also started laughing. He put his hand on the knee of the man next to him, and he began laughing uproariously, and touched the Pastor's wife on the shoulder. She began to laugh. Soon the seven in the room apart from Thelma and me were almost rolling on the floor with laughter, holding their sides.

I didn't feel at all amused, but thought "I can either sit here looking glum or at least try to laugh. "I'll try", so said "Ha, ha, ha, he, he, he, ho, ho, ho," and sounded so silly I began to giggle in spite of myself. This released the spirit of depression, which immediately left and soon both Thelma and I were laughing till our sides ached. "How wonderful, I haven't laughed like this for years", I thought, driving home.

However, the matter was not finished yet because some weeks later I was depressed again. This time I bought a book on "Spiritual Depression", which was written mainly around the verse from Ps 42:11:

"Why are you cast down O my soul, and why are you disquieted within me? Hope in God."

I became exasperated. "'O my soul!'. The man isn't talking about spiritual depression, this is the soul, the mind, not the spirit." God seemed to say "That's right, it's in your mind. You are depressed because you feel I have put you on the shelf and forgotten about you. Everyone is being blessed except you." I realised that this was right, I was depressed in the mind. I repented, asking the Lord to forgive me for not trusting Him, and asked Him to increase my faith.

He had shown me that the depression was on three levels, body, soul and spirit. After He had healed all three levels the depression left, never to return. We must remember when we minister to people that the depression is probably on three levels. It will not leave till all three have been healed if this is the case.

## Restoration

I realised that not only must I repent of backsliding, and turn from it, but I needed restoration. Jer 15: 19 RSV:

"If you return to me, I will *restore* you and *you shall stand before Me*".

Oh to be able to say as Elijah did "As the Lord God of Israel lives, *before Whom I stand*". I went forward for laying-on-of-hands for restoration, and that night as I turned over my Bible I came in three consecutive places to "I will restore you", "restore you", "restore". Praise God, I knew I was restored.

What I needed now was strength to walk in this closeness with the Lord, strength to break the relationship with Yohan.

## c) Parting with Yohan

The Holy Spirit had made it quite plain that Yohan and I must part, so he came to visit me for the last time, with a poem, a bunch of flowers, and his signet ring. The flowers were so beautiful, red roses, with the poem tucked in beside the flowers:

"My true love hath my heart and I have his,
By just exchange one for another given,
I hold his dear, and mine he cannot miss
There never was a better bargain driven.
My true-love hath my heart, and I have his.

His heart in me keeps him and me in one,
My heart in him his thoughts and senses guides.
He loves my heart, for once it was his own.
I cherish his because in me it bides,
My true-love hath my heart, and I have his."

Sir Philip Sydney.

He placed his ring on my finger and said "Keep this, I'll be back for it in God's time," but in my heart I knew the separation was to be complete, and returned the ring.

After he left I went into the bedroom, knelt to pray and cry before the Lord, and release him to the Lord in full commitment. I opened the Bible at Philemon, NEB (from v12, my prayer of release):

"I am sending him back to You, and in so doing I am sending a part of myself. I should have liked to keep him with me, to look after me ...... but I would rather do nothing without Your consent. ..... for perhaps this is why You lost him for a time, that You might have him back for good, no longer as a slave, but as more than a slave, as a dear brother, very dear indeed to me, and how much dearer to You both as man and as Christian ..... if he has done any wrong or is in Your debt, put that down to my account."

There was a current song that went something like this:

"Never again will I call to see you,
Never again will I drive past to see
if your light is still burning,
Never again will I hold you in my arms,
But I love you."

My God, how my heart aches.

"All to Jesus I surrender."

# PART THREE

# The Promised Land

# Chapter 10
# Crossing Jordan

## a) Baptism in the Holy Spirit

My heart was drawn to the joy and healing power found these days in the Charismatic Movement. I was seeking the Baptism in the Holy Spirit, so in January '73 I booked in as a delegate to the first National Charismatic Convention, held at NSW University. I listened keenly to the doctrine.

Having two Theology Diplomas through Moore College and Board of Education, I knew I'd recognise any heresy or errors, but after three days lectures agreed that the speakers were 'spot on'. The main difference from my denominational teaching was that they claimed to receive the Baptism in the Holy Spirit, in most cases by the laying-on-of-hands of believers. From this infilling the believer was now in a position to receive the gifts of the Spirit as spoken of in 1 Corinthians 12 and 14.

I was reading "Smith Wigglesworth, Apostle of Faith" about a renowned old Pentecostal who was a channel for much miracle power. The Holy Spirit showed me "You shall be baptised in the Holy Spirit according to Acts 2:4 not many days hence."

I was excited, and prayed for confirmation which I received in different ways, including a friend who came to me and said "My dear, you must be baptised in the Holy Spirit. I was baptised yesterday through a Presbyterian Minister from Victoria, and I spoke in tongues all night." I prayed that if it was the Lord's will I would see this minister in the crowd, and speak to him. At morning coffee break he was standing beside me sipping tea. I made arrangements to be prayed for by him and his wife after the evening meeting.

During the day I had misgivings, but the Lord encouraged, and when we gathered for prayer in the evening I was very excited. My friend who had spoken in tongues all night was also present.

The Rev. Robin Webb and his wife explained that Jesus was the Baptiser (according to Matthew 3:11, Mark 1:8, Luke 3:16, John 1:33), and that I would be filled with the Holy Spirit according to Acts 1:8:

"You shall receive power when the Holy Spirit has come upon you".

and Acts 2:4:

"And they were all filled with the Holy Spirit and began to speak with other tongues, as the Spirit gave them utterance."

Robin Webb asked me to pray for the infilling, and then he, his wife and my friend laid hands on my head and shoulders and began to pray for me, seated in a chair or "hot seat". They prayed earnestly for a long time, but absoutely nothing seemed to happen. When they finally ceased and said "How do you feel?' I felt quite a hopeless case, and said apologetically "Absolutely no different, I think I'm wasting your time. I'll go now and come back some other time."

Robin encouraged me back into the chair, and his wife said "I can feel the Holy Spirit going in through my hands, she really is receiving." He thought for a moment, and asked "Is there anything in your life that is coming between you and God? Any unconfessed sin?" I replied "I do have a problem over a relationship, but I'm prepared to do anything the Lord wants me to in the situation, and actually we've split up." Robin said "No, that's not it." Then "Sometimes at this stage people will either laugh or cry, depending on what has been going on in their lives." He laid hands on me again and prayed, and suddenly I threw back my head and gave a loud mocking laugh. Robin stepped back in shock, and consternation, as he recognised a mocking spirit leaving, stirred up by the Holy Spirit. He then said "OK, this is it", and began praying in tongues again.

Within less than a minute I began to feel the power of the Holy Spirit. I felt as though I was being filled up with "warm sparkling lemonade" from my hips (I was in the sitting position). This sparkling feeling slowly filled me up like a vessel. It moved up to the waist, the chest (where a lump in the breast disappeared miraculously at this moment), then the neck. I thought "As this fills my throat, my mouth, I'll begin speaking in tongues according to Acts 2:4. I began making "ahhhhhhh" noises trying to make tongues come more easily.

The feeling of "being filled' moved up the throat, but at the same time my ears blocked (being on a level with my mouth). Even though I knew my tongue was moving, I couldn't hear a thing. The spiritual "fulness" moved slowly to the top of my head, and then began to "lift off". My ears cleared, and I heard myself speaking in tongues (according to Acts 2:4).

The wonderful fulness of love which accompanies the Baptism in the Holy Spirit just flows from those who are filled with the Spirit, the true "living waters flowing from your innermost being". John 7:38. What a marvellous transformation, what a wonderful new life.

Oh the joy of the infilling of the Holy Spirit! Only those who have received it can know! We had hugs and laughs and praises and thanksgiving to Jesus for His wonderful gift. I could hardly believe it for joy. Robin said "Be careful! Until now you have been driving a Holden (as it were). Now you have a Masserati! It's a powerful vehicle you are handling now."

Praise You Father, Jesus, for the gift of the fulness of the Holy Spirit, for the Person I now know Who was hidden to me before.

I spoke in tongues all the way back to Lindfield in case I couldn't start again if I stopped. Indeed, the noises I was making were not at this time a language, but a series of sounds. They reminded me of the sounds the family budgie was making before he began speaking properly. I laughed at the thought. It was the Lord loosening up my tongue to express another language. Two or three days later the words began forming. By the end of the week the language with its sentences, exclamations etc. was there to stay. My prayer life was transformed into a wonderful love time with Jesus. As Jude says in v20:

"Building yourselves up on your most holy faith, praying in the Holy Spirit."

Jesus, if those who don't speak with tongues only knew what they were missing!"

I simply could not contain this new-found fulness, and rang the curate to share with him. He came to my home that afternoon to hear of this wonderul new experience. I had read 1 Corinthians 12 and 14 again, and was amazed at what I saw there. The Curate was puzzled. I read extracts from these chapters saying excitedly "Just listen to this ...... I never saw this before. Look what this says .....", but the Curate said soberly "Ruth, that has always been there, why haven't you noticed it?" I realised that his eyes were still blind, he just wasn't seeing what the Holy Spirit was saying in this passage.

A veil had been lifted from my eyes in the Baptism experience. "This one thing I know, whereas I was blind, now I see". This veil still hangs over the eyes of the denominational churches, and until they reach out for the Baptism they will not be able to see. The Curate left rather sadly, puzzled and a little irritated. In his mind I was no longer 'one of us', but had become 'one of them'.

I continued to take Communion at my local church for a further eighteen months, and witnessed constantly, but seemingly in vain. The Minister, although he knew there was something in the Charismatic Movement, and admitted as much, still didn't enquire into it. I do believe that our leaders are like the ten spies who were sent out by Moses to sum up possibilities in the Promised Land. "They did not enter in because of UNBELIEF". This unbelief is largely due to ignorance, because they don't want to know. "There is none so blind as those who will not see."

I was eventually shown by the Lord to leave the local church, and joined a Spirit-filled group, Christian Faith Centre at Lane Cove. This group later moved to St. Leonards.

I will never forget the thrill of the new services, hearing the Congregation singing spontaneously, beautiful choruses like:

"My Beloved spake and said unto me,
Rise up My love, My fair one, and come away,
For lo the winter is passed, the rain is over and gone,
The flowers appear on the earth,
The singing of birds is at hand,
And the voice of the turtle is heard in our land."

All were standing, hands raised in love and surrender to Jesus, eyes closed, hearts full of joy and love. They then moved by the Spirit into spiritual worship, singing a new song in tongues to the Lord. So exhilirating and satisfying!

After receiving the fulness of the Spirit Christians nearly always face a 'Jericho'. When the children of Israel entered the Promised Land, and were totally set apart to the Lord, they sighted the seemingly impregnable walls of Jericho.

My Jericho was my love for Yohan, to whom I was still emotionally bound. He rang occasionally and finally said "I can't live without you any longer, may I come and see you?" Weakly I said "It's been so long, just this once."

We had a precious day together, but that night the Lord spoke to my spirit saying "I have come to the end of My patience with you. This is it! If you don't stop this relationship right now, as you swore to me you would, he will die, and you will finish up in Psychiatric Hospital. Beware that you are not a 'profane person like Esau, who for a mouthful of pottage sold his birthright'".

The very next day news came through that Yohan was gravely ill in hospital, not expected to live. It was ten days before he was out of intensive care, during which time he could have died at any moment. There was absolutely no doubt now, the relationship was finished, finished. We hear about the "fear of God", and these are not idle words. God says what He means, and He means what He says. I prayed for forgiveness and restoration in awe and true repentance.

## b) Repentance

This is a gift. We can't always choose to repent just when it is convenient for us. Sometimes, as with Esau, repentance is witheld from us. Esau had remorse, but no repentance, though "he sought it with tears". God was saying here, "This is your final chance for true repentance Ruth, this is the end of My patience." And I knew that this was FINAL.

Scriptures were given at Service on Sunday which totally confirmed this, including the verse and chorus from Galatians 5:1:

"Stand fast therefore in the liberty by which Christ has made us free, and do not be entangled again with a yoke of bondage."

## c) Rebellion

I was teaching in Scripture lessons about the walls of Jerusalem being broken down by sin, and realised that due to my backsliding, the walls of my life were broken down. I repented and prayed "Lord, like the walls of Jerusalem, break me down and start again." This prayer opened me almost to the verge of a nervous breakdown, but thank God it also led to my healing.

The Lord spoke quite clearly to my spirit and said "I can't build anything on you, because down in the foundation of your life is rebellion. I tried before to build an edifice on you, but you became rebellious and threw the whole thing away (not unlike a donkey kicking the cart to pieces). I can do nothing with you while the rebellion is still there. Also, you are anti-submissive, you won't submit to authority. How can I ever give you authority if you don't submit to it yourself?"

I repented of rebellion. All my life I'd been proud of being a rebel. At school I was often "on the mat" for rebellious behaviour, and the headmistress said on one occasion "There is a rebellious element in this class, and you, Ruth, are the ringleader." But now I said, "I renounce all rebellion Lord, I want to be a comformist." (The word conformist nearly choked me - I was proud of being a rebel). "I want to be able to say "I delight to do Your will, O my God."

From that moment the rebellion left, and I decided to submit (as much as I knew to be right) to delegated authority. This was a hard one, but I prayed "Lord, as long as I know the person in authority is under You, doing You will Your way, I will submit."

## d) Water Baptism

When it was announced at Church that there would be a Water Baptism in the Lane Cove River a friend asked if I planned to be baptised. I had been sprinkled in the best Anglican tradition as a baby, and immersion had never crossed my mind, but someone pointed out that Jesus Himself was immersed. As He was an example to us in all things, it behoves us to "fulfil all righteousness." Rather than disobey I agreed.

The family objected strongly, my Mother saying that she feared for my sanity. Not wanting to fall short of the Lord's requirements I went ahead. The children thought this all rather strange, and weren't interested in coming, although James and a friend hired canoes and paddelled around at a distance to watch. We all put on long white baptismal robes and stood around looking a little like angels, much to the interest and amusement of picnickers at the Lane Cove National Park. We stepped one at a time into the water and two pastors, one on either side, prayed for us and lowered us under.

Water Baptism, immersion, is a symbolic burial of the old dead life and a rising again to resurrection life of the new person in Christ. We were taught to recognise all the old bad habits, sins, negative reactions, dead and buried. Being renewed in Christ, we were to reckon ourselves released from them and healed and cleansed for a new resurrection walk.

It was a tremendous experience, and a great spiritual advance. I was a new person with a new inner strength after this. I recognise that there are three main Christian steps:

1. To be 'Born Again' by receiving Jesus as Saviour and Lord.
2. Baptism in water, immersion as a burial into Christ and a witness to our 'Born Again' experience.
3. Baptism in the Holy Spirit.

The three steps may occur almost simultaneously. A Born-again believer may say "I now want to be baptised according to my new faith". As the Ethiopian eunuch in Acts, we may be immersed immediately or as in Acts 16:33:

"And immediately he and all his family were baptised".

Many come up out of the water filled with the Holy Spirit and speaking in tongues. On the other hand the steps may be years apart, as mine were. I was fifteen years in the 'Born Again' experience. After this came the Baptism in the Holy Spirit, and eleven months later Baptism by immersion. Don't miss any of these steps, they are a must!

I was amazed at the new teaching on healing. I had attended Church and Bible Study regularly in the denominational Church, knew the Word, doctrine etc., but was torn apart by unhealed emotions.

One particular sermon stuck in my mind on "Entering the Promised Land". When we enter the Promised Land, which is our full inheritance in Christ, we need to leave behind our old hangups and negative reactions which will only ruin our new life. Things like Rejection, Fear of Rejection, Poor Self Image, Insecurity, Rebellion, Resentment etc. must go. Jesus heals as well as forgives. Matt 8:17:

"He Himself took our infirmities, and bore our sicknesses."

Is 53:5: "By His stripes we are healed".

1 Pet 2:24 "By Whose stripes you were healed."

# Chapter 11
# My Jericho

## Affliction - I need a man

On one memorable occasion at Church the Pastor said "Let's all stand, and lift our hearts to the Lord, and whatever your need, pour it out to Him." Tears were streaming down by face as I prayed "Please Lord, I need a man, Your man for me, a Christian husband. I've waited so long. Lord, either fill this void in my heart with Yourself and your love, or give me a Christian husband."

Arriving home I opened the Bible and read Job 36:15 RSV:

"He delivers the afflicted by their affliction and opens their ear by adversity.'

In other words "You are afflicted, I acknowledge that, but I am delivering you from all your hang-ups and from things that would hurt you. In this adversity you have an open ear to Me. In prosperity you are more self-sufficient, but in adversity you wait on Me and listen to Me."

I felt He was also saying "No, I'm not going to fill your heart with Myself, nor am I giving you a man at this stage. You hear me better when you are in need." The disappointment that the time had not yet arrived for marriage was surpassed by the joy and love of a faithful, all-knowing, all-loving God.

About this time I received a prophecy:

"I am allowing these things to happen to you so that you will know what is in your heart. I know

107

what is in your heart, but I want you to know it too."

Jeremiah says in 17:9:

"The heart is deceitful above all things, and desperately wicked; who can know it?'

You know it Lord. Please give me a pure heart, help me to overcome and become more like Jesus."

## Rejection, Insecurity

I felt as though I was stripped down to nothing in my personality, facing up to the fact that there was so much rejection in my life, that I was beginning to feel unsure of myself in relating to people, insecure, with a fear of being rejected, and a poor self image, low self esteem. For the self-sufficient person I had been to now feel these uncomfortable reactions was devestating.

But this is how the Lord works in our lives. It has been said that "the way up is down". This is often true! We must face up to the fact that "In me dwells no good thing", and be prepared to submit to the hands of the Potter. Only He knows what type of vessel he is making. Our part is to hang in there, submit and trust Him, a faithful and loving God. He is the Rebuilder of Broken Walls, and hadn't I prayed "Break me up and start again?"

# Chapter 12
# Visit To Israel

At about this time I received in the mail a brochure from Logos Ministries regarding a trip to Israel to celebrate the first Worldwide Convention of the Outpouring of the Holy Spirit. It was to be held at the season of Pentecost. "I wonder if I could attend that?" The Lord gave me a few signs that this was available to me.

Arriving early for the morning meeting I sat in the car, prayed for guidance, and opened the Bible at Isaiah 33. It all seemed to be "Woe, woe, woe", until suddenly the verses 17, 19, 20, 21 gripped me:

> "Your eyes will see the King in His beauty, they will see the land that is very far off.
>
> v20 Look upon Zion, the city of our appointed feasts; *your eyes will see Jerusalem,*
>
> v21 But there the majestic Lord will be for us a place of broad rivers and streams" (talking about the outpouring of the Holy Spirit.)

Even v19 "You will not see a fierce people, a people of obscure speech, beyond perception, of a stammering tongue that you cannot understand" seemed to me to be speaking of tongues, which was one of the principal features of the Convention.

Praise God, I can go!

When I entered the Church the congregation was singing "Let's go up to Zion", and the sermon was on the "Let's go up to Zion" theme. How about the children? This meant leaving the household in Julia's charge once more; Julia was now 23, and Lindsay was studying abroad. The morning I left the Lord gave the verse from Job 5:24 Living Bible:

"You need not worry about your home when you are gone, nothing shall be stolen from your barns."

God had also spoken to me from Isaiah 34:15,16:

"Every one with her mate" and "None shall lack her mate", and I was excited. "Will I meet my husband in Jerusalem, Lord?"

What a wonderful privilege to visit the Holy Land! And Jerusalem! Of all the cities in the world the greatest by far is Jerusalem! The city of our God! Even the cats were exhilarated the morning I left, racing around the house and finally sitting together watching as the luggage was loaded, and I drove off. They knew something important was happening.

The flight was tiring but what a thrill to stand on Israeli soil! I felt I was on holy ground.

When we drove up from the Airport at Tel Aviv to the City, rounding a bend we saw Jerusalem in all her glory. The bus driver stopped the bus and we just sat there in wonder. I doubt if there was a dry eye. There is just something about Jerusalem, and of course that something is Someone, Jesus. Even though the Old City has changed since He walked the streets, He is still there, walking in those who have yielded their hearts and lives to Him.

I had many spiritual experiences whilst in Israel. We visited the Lithostrum on the Via Dolorosa (The Way of the Cross), and sat listening to the guide. He explained that this was where Jesus was scourged, stripped, dressed in the scarlet robe, mocked, spat upon and buffetted, and then lead away to die. Grooves in the floor show where the Roman Soldiers played their dice games.

I was sitting talking to Jesus and saying "Lord,

You are here again in me". I remembered the buffetting etc., and shed a few tears. A lady with a heavy carry-bag climbed over the seat beside me, hitting me on the ear with such a blow that my ear tingled. The weight knocked my head sideways, a little reminder of what Jesus suffered there. The lady didn't apologise or even look at me, and I had a taste of the rejection of Jesus as well.

We moved from this room to the Via Dolorosa, where another amazing thing happened. There was a dear little grey donkey pulling an enormous weight of steel reinforcing. It was strapped to his back and dragged along the ground behind him. As he struggled with the load down the Via Dolorosa, his feet slipped on the stones with the weight. A man walked alongside whipping the donkey, shouting at him to keep going. The Pastor standing next to me remonstrated with the owner, an Arab, who spat in his face and snarled "Go home, Christian."

I protested "What a cruel, sadistic thing to do to that dear little donkey, the weight is far too heavy for him." The pastor said "Who do you think should carry it, the man or the donkey?" I retorted "The man." Jesus whispered "I carried the Cross along this street for you. It was heavy." "Lord, thankyou for carrying the Cross for me. Thankyou too for showing me the pathos of it through this little donkey."

Aren't the Lord's ways just wonderful!

Another experience, this time at the tomb. A few of us were gathered together at the Garden Tomb, in the sepulchre itself. I looked at the stone platform where the body of Jesus is thought to have laid, but had no feeling of His presence. I was feeling quite disappointed till someone spoke firmly in the stillness of the tomb "He is not here, He is risen". "Of course You are not in the tomb Jesus, You are risen, risen indeed."

We were to cross the Sea of Galilee from Tiberias to Capernaum on a little launch on another memorable occasion. The usually calm, sparkling waters were grey and troubled, the sea quite choppy. We put out from the shore, but the storm was approaching quickly, tossing and rolling the boat until the Captain announced that the storm would endanger the crossing. We turned back. It was interesting to experience a storm and imagine the disciples and Jesus tossed and nearly swamped. This was the only storm I've seen on Galilee, thankyou Jesus for the experience.

Perhaps the most thrilling event was on the last day in Jerusalem, when we moved into a Hotel built adjacent to Calvary, the place of a skull. My bedroom window looked onto the hill, a stone's throw away. I was praying at the window when Mary, a mature Christian with a deliverance ministry came in and asked "May I pray with you? I feel you could do with some deliverance."

We prayed together and Mary commanded spirits of insecurity, confusion and hate to leave, in Jesus' Name. She asked that He heal me of hurts I had suffered in the past. Mary said "Now lift your hands and tell the Lord you love Him", and I couldn't! I simply could not raise my arms. "I can't". She prayed again, and suddenly my arms were released, and I was able to raise them and praise my God. Great joy filled my heart, the spirits had gone, the hurts were healed.

We danced and sang and laughed. Afterwards as I looked out the window, I realised the significance of my first deliverance. It was at Calvary! It was here Jesus died that we might be forgiven, healed, released from our bondages. Here He overcame all that Satan inflicts on us, and went on to the grave and Hell to overcome death. "I have the keys of Death and Hell", said the triumphant Jesus. Thankyou Lord for Your great deliverance. If only people knew the truth, that they can be set free by You and You alone. Hallelujah!

All the time in Jerusalem I'd been wondering where my Christian husband was, and as the days passed I became disappointed and disillusioned. Then the Lord spoke and said "Are you going to let the Devil snatch away the joy of this time with Me in My city, My Promised Land?" I realised Satan was trying to undercut my faith, and told the Lord I didn't mind about the husband, He was more than enough.

The promise "Not one will be there without her mate" was a puzzle, actually fulfilled on my second visit to Israel when I travelled there on my honeymoon. Sometimes the fulfilment of a prophecy is a little further ahead than we anticipate. Thankyou Jesus, You were right all the time.

# Kathryn Kuhlman

On the final day of the Convention Kathryn Kuhlman spoke and ministered. What an experience! The meeting was reasonably uneventful until the power of the Holy Spirit fell, and from that moment - DRAMA!

"There is a lady in the gallery, you are being healed, you were born deaf in one ear, God is opening that ear, come down to the platform and tell us about it". "A man over here (pointing), in a brace, a lower spinal injury is being healed, remove the brace and come down to give thanks to Jesus. A boy over there, nearly blind, Jesus is healing your eyes, come down to the platform."

This went on and on, with a stream of people being

healed and moving to the front of the Auditorium. At the foot of the stairs leading up to the platform was a medical doctor checking on the healings before letting anyone up there to testify. The boy, whose glasses were incredibly thick, spoke to Kathryn Kuhlman. She gave him a Bible and he read a long passage without glasses, completely healed. Someone called out from the Congregation "May I have a look at the glasses?" His father, who was with the boy, called back, "You can have them."

People were waving their braces in the air, others were getting out of wheelchairs, some were shouting praises to God as they realised they were healed, running around the hall, out to the front. Others were touching their toes, swinging their bodies from side to side, rolling their heads around as their necks were healed. The meeting which had been like any sedate Christian meeting now seemed to be in a state of chaos, such is the liberating power of God.

On the platform Kathryn was speaking to those who came to testify. The healings were all done in the body of the hall by the power of the Spirit. The only time she touched the people was in blessing, after they told what God had done in their lives. When she touched them the power of the Holy Spirit was so great that they immediately fell to the floor. As many as she touched went down under the power. It seemed as though the power flowing through her was almost too great to contain. She'd often say "Oh, the power of the Holy Ghost", and touch about five or six people or more in quick succession, and they would fall like ninepins. It was as though the buildup of power in her hands must be discharged.

She then said "Now, I'll walk through the body of the hall. DO NOT reach out and touch me." As she walked, followed by a group of ministers, whole rows of the congregation fell to the ground. Uncanny! What power lies in the Holy Spirit! We cannot begin to comprehend the power of God.

We had all hoped that perhaps there would be a repeat of the "rushing mighty wind" of the Holy Spirit. It was the largest Christian gathering in Jerusalem since Pentecost, but in spite of the spectacular healings and miracles, no "rushing, mighty wind".

Kathryn ministered again in the final evening meeting with more tremendous healings and miracles, but this was not the occasion for another Pentecostal outpouring as in the Upper Room.

# Chapter 13
# Battles and Blessings

## a) Sealed Orders

Agnes Sanford wrote an autobiography called "Sealed Orders" in which she explained that during wartime the Captain of a Ship receives "Sealed Orders" regarding destination etc. The envelope containing the orders is delivered to the ship by the staff of Naval Command. It is locked in the ship's safe, in the presence of the Captain. These Orders are only to be opened when the ship is ten miles out to sea, to prevent leakage of important information which might sabotage the ship.

Agnes Sanford said "Until now, I didn't know the Sealed Orders with which I came to this earth." This saying caught my imagination. "What are my Sealed Orders? Why am I here? What is the prime purpose God has for me? Please Lord, reveal Your Sealed Orders for my life."

Christian Faith Centre had a vision for setting up a "Hot Line" or 24-hour telephone counselling line, and Pastor Harold Dewberry was asked to train the first group of Counsellors. I was a counsellor on Lifeline, and didn't want to be further committed, but a friend, Joyce, asked me to attend the meeting where the setting up of Crisis Call was to be discussed. I sat in the back of the room, determined to say nothing, and not become involved. This was quite successful until one minute before the meeting closed, and someone said "Ruth works on Lifeline".

After closing the meeting the Pastor approached

me about helping start the new service, and I gave the guarded Christian reply "I'll pray about it". I asked the Lord for guidance.

A prophecy was given at the Sunday morning meeting about walking on the water. Jesus said "Come", and I felt He was speaking to me, but I really didn't want to "come" at all.

Later at home, when reading Psalm 119, I asked "If You want me on Crisis Call, please give me the word "Come". Psalm 119 is mainly about the law, testimonies, statutes etc. and I felt quite safe, when suddenly verse 48, Living Bible, appeared:

"Come, come to Me. I call to them".

"Come" not once, but twice, which always has the sense of imperative about it in the Bible. I knew in my heart this was the verification of my call to Crisis Call. It proved to be my Sealed Orders, a call now thirteen years old, and still Jesus calls "Come to Me, walk on the water."

The Sealed Orders also encompass the writing of this book. Agnes Sanford was told in her "Sealed Orders" to write two hours a day following a manic depressive breakdown. The doctor asked "What do you like to do?" "Write". "I suggest you write for two hours every day. Employ a babysitter if necessary, but this is part of your healing, your emotions will be released as you write."

Part of my Sealed Orders is to write this account of my Christian walk. In 1958 Jesus showed me to begin keeping a spiritual diary, which contains the subject matter for this book.

## b) Crisis Call

There had been an initial attempt to open Crisis Call in March '74, precipitated by the filming of "The

Exorcist" in Sydney. It was felt that the film might open people to spiritual confusion and many questions would be asked. Pamphlets were distributed outside the Theatre giving a telephone number with a "Please call us if you are disturbed" message. Many rang, and at least one gave his heart to Jesus. After six weeks the service closed down. On the tenth of June, 1974, Crisis Call St. Leonards began operating under a new number which appeared inside the cover of every telephone book in Sydney. From here on it was a 24-hour service.

The Lord spoke during the night to my spirit and said "Operate the resources and information as a 3-coloured card system, yellow for telephone numbers, addresses and practical information for contacting referrals etc., green cards for counselling procedures and grey for additional information which would be helpful to the Counsellor.

eg. ALCOHOL

Yellow card - Phone No's of Alcoholics Anonymous, Al Anon etc., clinics for drying out, rehabilitation etc.

Green card - Possible counselling proceedures

Grey card - Further information about Alcohol, its effects etc.

On the Sunday before the service began the Holy Spirit spoke clearly through Genesis 17:1:

"Walk before Me and be blameless"

and I dedicated my life afresh to the service of God.

As Crisis Call grew, so did the resources etc., but this was how we began. The devil didn't want me to continue with this walk, and I had at this time a proposal of marriage by a dedicated Christian widower, but I knew he wasn't the right one. I had my eyes now on Jesus, and was learning to walk on the water.

118

## c) Demon Possession

The devil had another attempt to lure me off the path. On one occasion at midnight the overnight counsellor rang to say in a choked voice that there was trouble at the office, which was located in the church building. She had admitted a woman to the premises about midnight (strictly against the rules). The woman was now becoming quite violent, threatening to break all the windows in the building with her shoe.

I drove down to confronted by a wild-eyed lesbian 'butch' who decided she would attack me as well. (Rolph, our male overseer, was away for the weekend). The woman was demon possessed. I informed her that Jesus in me was far stronger then the spirit in her and to pull herself together and leave the building. She grabbed hold of a big screen on shepherd's castors and began pushing it at me, till I ordered her in the name of Jesus to stop.

She then walked over to me, eyes blazing with hate and demon spirits, put her face close to mine and looking straight in my eyes the demon spoke, "You need a man, I'll give you a man. He'll have every semblance of being a Christian. He'll attend meetings with you. I'll give you a man if you'll only do what I say". I replied, "I don't want any man you would give me, I'll have the man the Lord gives me."

The devil, up to his old tricks again, trying to bargain with a child of God. It reminds one of the temptation in the wilderness "All these things will I give You if You'll fall down and worship me."

At this stage I was not confident in the deliverance ministry, so was too unsure of myself to bind the demon or command it to depart. It recognised the Holy Spirit in me however, because when the woman was commanded in the name of Jesus to leave the building she went quietly.

## d) Fellowship Group

I was asked to lead a Fellowship Group and resisted strongly, realising that I was not yet capable of moving in the Spirit.

In the denominational churches these things are relatively simple. One works out a programme and follows it. There will usually be a central theme, Bible study, discussion etc., and perhaps formal prayers, but a Spirit-filled group is a different matter.

I realised my short-comings. One generally begins with singing, praise and worship, moving into singing and speaking in tongues, with maybe the Holy Spirit giving a new spiritual song, prophecy or a tongues message with interpretation. A Bible study or message may then be given, or discussion, followed by invitation for anyone wanting prayer for healing, relationship or financial problems, and perhaps even deliverance or Baptism in the Holy Spirit.

I just didn't feel up to this, but the Pastors of the church felt I was, and insisted. Submitting to delegated authority I ran a group, but when Doug Spencer asked if he could join I felt threatened and said "No way, no men in my group." (Some of the young men in the church felt threatened by women teachers, so I banned all males.)

## e) The Occult

After our eyes are opened by the Baptism in the Holy Spirit, we see much deeper into the spirit realm.

One of the gifts of the Spirit is discerning of spirits. Through this gift we now understand that not only are we greatly swayed by our thinking, by our memories, but also spiritual forces within and without. Some of these spiritual pressures come from personality defects. For example, reactions built up in the mind and the heart by things like resentment, un-forgiveness, bitterness, anger, dominant spirit, rebellion, self-will, pride, jealousy, suspicion, dis-trust, fears, rejection, insecurity, inferiority, self-condemnation, self-consciousness etc.

Many of these reactions are only in the mind, but others are in both mind and heart. The heart and spirit are very close, though not synonomous. It has been said that "As the mind is the seat of the soul, so is the heart the seat of the spirit." This seems quite a good explanation, although not totally accurate. It is a very broad subject, and I just want to touch on the essential difference between the soul and the spirit.

There are however, forces in the Occult which have a bearing on our behaviour and our thinking. These may be inherited or acquired during our lives.

I had inherited through my paternal grandmother. occult powers of which I was totally unaware until I received the gift of discerning of spirits. When we visited my grandmother she always held my face with a hand on each cheek (which I hated) and kissed me soundly. After tea and cake she'd read my teacup, palm and finally produce the cards and read the future (often at my request). I liked this, it was exciting to know the future.

She was a strange woman. Her wedding present to my mother was a stuffed eagle in a glass case, sitting on coral. My mother hated it, and kept it in a cup-board, only to be placed on a table in the hall when grandma was expected to visit. Apparently g'ma was a practicing medium, because she tried to arrange a seance in a hall in Chatswood, presenting herself as the medium. She wanted my father to print pamphlets advertising this seance, which she intended to hand out on a street corner. Daddy refused.

I had experienced three premonitions of death, some clairvoyance, but this I attributed largely to "a women's intuition", and it didn't concern me greatly. Ignorance is bliss! The thought that occult powers inherited from g'ma were affecting my life would never have entered my head, but the Holy Spirit revealed this to me later as I learned more about the powers of darkness.

Feeling a certain frustration in my Crisis Call work, I went to Rolph, pastor in charge of counselling. Several spirits like self-consciousness, frustration, intolerance, impatience were discerned, repented of and cast out, and the oppression left. A feeling of freedom and joy entered my soul, I was released. What I had to do from then on was to exercise love, where I used to react in frustration and intolerance.

However, there was something else there, and for the next three days I had constant indigestion, burping all day. I never suffer from indigestion, so mentioned this to Rolph, who said "It may be a tummy wog. I'll pray for healing, but if you're still burping tomorrow it'll no doubt be a spirit ."

The following day I was still burping. Rolph said, "I don't know what it is, pray and see if the Holy Spirit will tell you." I asked the Lord to reveal to me what the spirit was, and as I was wrapping the rubbish in newspaper that night a heading caught my eye, and witnessed with my spirit. The heading was "Death Wish", the name of a film being advertised for a Sydney Theatre. The Holy Spirit said to my spirit "You have a Death Wish".

# f) Death Wish

I had noticed a few times in the last few years that

the thought of "dying and getting away from it all" seemed to easiest way out, although I've never thought of suicide. Often when driving past a cemetery the verse in Revelation came to me:

"Blessed are the dead who die in the Lord from now on. 'Yes' says the Spirit, 'that they may rest from their labours, and their works follow them'." Rev 14:13

I knew in my heart I had a lot to do here before I joined them, sleeping peacefully in their beds, but it appealed to me in a wry type of humour.

So it was a Death Wish!

Rolph was amazed, placed his hands on my head and commanded the Death Wish and Spirit of Death to leave. As he gave this command in the name of Jesus, I experienced a release, the death wish had gone for ever. He also prayed for release from any occult powers inherited from g'ma, and they have never returned.

There was an amazing sequel to this story. A few weeks later Rolph came to me and said "There is a girl in my church office who has just undergone heavy deliverance. Would you go in and sit with her? I have to conduct the service in the church."

When I entered the office the girl, also named Ruth, was crouched over a radiator, face as pale a death, shaking all over. I knew her well and when I saw the freezing state she was in, put my arms around her and comforted and warmed her, holding her ice-cold hands in mine. "You've just had deliverance Ruth, do you mind telling me what it was you were delivered from?"

"A spirit of death" she said.

How amazing! No wonder she was cold. The spirit was manifesting (doing its thing), on the way out, and she was exhibiting the pallour and clammy cold of a corpse. I held her close for about fifteen minutes until the warmth came back into her body. How strange that Rolph (who had completely forgotten my death spirit experience), should ask me (also named Ruth), to comfort and support this girl. Thankyou Lord, Your ways are perfect, and past finding out.

I had had further dealings with the Occult which had to be faced and repented of, and forgiveness asked for, because Occult involvement is tantamount to turning to gods other than our Almighty God, and invokes a curse (Deut 29). I was never intentionally involved in witchcraft, satanism, psychic healing or mind control, mantras, meditation, seances etc., but other lesser things also open us to the Occult realm; things like reading horoscopes in magazines, newspapers, palm reading, fortune telling by cards, tarot cards, crystal balls, ouija boards, pendulums (eg. the spinning wedding ring on a thread over a pregnant woman's tummy), water divining, especially in the country, ESP party games etc.

All these bring us under the influence of Occult spirits and may give rise to fear, confusion, anxiety, headaches, nightmares, inability to read or study the Bible, depression, uncontrollable evil thoughts, and other things far, far worse which I won't mention here.

If you have been involved in any of these Occult practices you should consult a Spirit-filled counsellor or pastor who will help free you from them. You can't just ignore it and hope it'll go away - it won't!

## g) Kihilla

Our fellowship group went to Kihilla Convention Centre for a weekend of togetherness. Rolph was the group leader. I soon realised that there were seven married couples - and me! How alone I felt! Rolph said "Tonight I'm going to pray for you as couples. Each couple is to sit together, and Ruth, you sit over here!"

Talk about rubbing it in!

I drove down to Echo Point and in exasperation called "Lord, what are doing to me? All these loving couples make me feel so wretched and alone. God, if You only realised how lonely I am".

Silence! Then the still small Voice in my spirit "You have resentment towards me because I haven't given you a Christian husband. "Lord, forgive me, I didn't realise I had resentment towards You, I love You, truly I do. I renounce all desire for marriage, I belong to You alone, I'll never ask for a husband again."

I felt released in spirit and happily rejoined the group.

That night Rolph prophesied over each couple and when he laid hands on my head, the Holy Spirit spoke:

"You have moved in the flesh and strength of your own will. I have laughed to see your attempts to achieve your own ends. You have become discouraged at other times and turned aside from My purposes for you.

Forget the past. I have been forming you. You will be strong, a warrior, with an axe, chopping your way ahead, fearless, strong. I have used you as a man, but you have the heart and emotions of a woman.

I will come to you. I will be your Husband, and you will know Me in a way and in a closeness that very few will ever know. Your life is a parable. You will understand when you see it. I will give you discernment,"

If the Lord had not spoken to me a few hours earlier at Echo Point, and I had not repented of resentment and told Him I gave up all thought of marriage, I could never have received this prophecy. Praise God, His timing is perfect.

## h) Parable of "Ruth"

Just a very short version of the parable of "Ruth" as revealed to me by the Holy Spirit. Ruth of course being from the book of that name in the Bible.

Ruth lived in a heathen land, far from the God of Israel. (This is our condition in life before we know God). She married and was widowed after ten years, as I was. She followed Naomi (a believer) to Israel after the death of her husband. Ruth 1:16:

"Entreat me not to leave you, or to turn back from following after you; wherever you go, I will go; and wherever you lodge, I will lodge; your people shall be my people, and your God my God. Where you die, I will die, and there will I be buried. The Lord do so to me, and more also, if anything but death parts you and me."

Ruth came to believe in God "Under Whose wings you have come for refuge". Ruth 2:12.

Ruth married Boaz, (Jesus), and produced a son, Obed (Crisis Call). The Lord later gave me a physical representative of Himself, but I'll speak more about this later.

The parable goes deeper, but that is all I want to point out here.

## i) Douglas joins Crisis Call

A few months after my Kihilla experience, Doug Spencer was attempting to recruit counsellors for Crisis Call, with no success. When he was praying about it the Lord said "How about you?" Doug replied "I'm out so much now, with work pressures, meetings, etc., already I don't spend enough time with my family." "How about Wednesday nights?" "I'll talk to Mabs, Lord".

Mabs, Doug's wife, said "You are out Wednesday evenings already, so to do an overnight shift on Wednesdays would make no difference. We don't see you that night anyway."

Doug rang to say he'd tried to recruit counsellors without success, but he could do one night. The only overnight vacancy happened to be a Wednesday, so Doug took this as a sign from the Lord and joined the team.

He'd only been with us two weeks when a most horrific situation arose. A lady caller rang to say she had purchased a gun with the intention of shooting her four children and herself. She had levelled the gun at the sleeping children's heads, but it wouldn't fire. She wouldn't give her name or address. Doug counselled her for some time, but she was intent on carrying out her threat, and finally hung up.

The following night she did manage to fire the gun, and the evening paper carried the headlines "Woman shoots four children and herself".

My heart sank. How will Doug cope with this? Actually it was through this tragic case that God laid Crisis Call on Doug's heart, and he began to assume a responsible role in an advisory capacity, as well as counsellor.

At this stage of Crisis Call's life the Church finances took a downward plunge and Rolph had no alternative but to leave his pastoring position and seek secular employment. The church building housing Crisis Call was sold and Christian Faith Centre moved to Wahroonga, It was not advisable to move the Crisis

Centre so far from the City. As the phone number could also not be changed, being prominently displayed in every telephone book, we had no alternative but to remain at St. Leonards. We could not risk suicidal callers ringing a disconnected number, lives could be lost. New premises must be found.

Shortly after Crisis Call was settled into its new quarters, another tragic event. Doug's wife Mabs died suddenly from a heart attack. She'd had no indication of heart trouble, and the doctor, when called, thought it was indigestion pain, or something minor. Doug was greatly shocked, and left us for a few weeks, concentrating on looking after his three daughters.

# Chapter 14
# Town Hall Healing

Francis and Charles Hunter were ministering healing at the Sydney Town Hall, and I attended with a friend. During the meeting Charles asked all present with knee trouble to stand. We were to move into the aisle and swing our leg at the knee until it was healed, and then when we knew it was healed to sit down. When all except three had been healed (forty in all), he asked the three remaining standing to come up on the platform.

Up we went! Charles asked me "What's the trouble?" and I replied "It's not just my knee, I need a healing of varicose veins." Charles said "Varicose veins! That's easy", and touched me lightly just below each knee. The Holy Spirit came upon me and I fell unconscious to the floor "out in the Spirit".

When I awoke I was lying on the Town Hall platform (with the two others he'd called), and Francis and Charles were conducting the meeting dodging our supine bodies.

My first thought was "What on earth will I do? If I try to get up I'll make more of a disturbance than just lying here quietly," so I lay still. Then the Holy Spirit said to my spirit "I am giving you a total healing, not just your veins, but your heart as well, your whole vascular system". I had been breathless after exertion lately and knew my heart wasn't the best. Suddenly it began to pound and thump and I felt as though I was going to have a heart attack. It pumped wildly for two or three minutes and then settled down, completely healed. There has been no more undue puffing ever since.

When the meeting was over and we three on the platform struggled groggily to our feet, still under the power of the Spirit, the TV cameras homed in on us. An interviewer asked if we were healed, how we felt, were we hypnotised? Yes, we were healed, the Holy Spirit doesn't go to all that trouble for nothing. No, we were not hypnotised. Hypnosis is of the Occult.

My heart has never given me any trouble since, neither have the varicose veins. The lumps didn't disappear, but I've had no pains, cramps or other discomfort since, and that was eleven years ago.

# Chapter 15
# A New Marriage

And still Crisis Call claimed my almost undivided attention. It was like a baby, a 24-hour responsibility. Praise God we had good faithful counsellors, but the work must be co-ordinated and supervised, counsellors trained and encouraged.

Family matters also keep one occupied. Julia, my second daughter was married about this time, and I dealt with the one-hundred-and-one things one does as mother of the bride.

With the shared interest of the running of Crisis Call, it was not surprising that after a few months a romantic attachment sprang up between Doug and me. We attended a meeting where the Holy Spirit revealed we were to be married. Is 62:4:

"Hepzibah, Beulah, for the Lord delights in you that you should be married."

was the new chorus we learned at this time.

I also received a brochure about Israel in the post, and realised that this was where we were to spend our honeymoon. The Lord verified this in many different ways.

## Marriage

So on the 3rd November, 1976, Doug and I were married after the Wednesday night Healing Service at St. Andrew's Cathedral. The following is an extract from Church Scene headed "Every Cathedral should have one", written by Marjorie Hawken.

"A square 'does' something for a cathedral. And

now Sydney has joined the ranks of famous cathedrals that have one…"

Marjorie goes on to say:

"In the presence of the usual large congregation of about 700 or 800 who attend the weekly Healing Service, there was a marriage. Douglas Spencer and Ruth Halliday, both regular participators in the Wednesday service, were married by the Rev. Canon Jim Glennon, who conducts the Healing Ministry. Afterwards, the simple refreshments in the Chapter House became a much more elaborate wedding breakfast, to which all were invited. Could this be the beginning of a new trend? Can we expect to see more weddings taking place before the whole Church family? 'Togetherness' is becoming more important in the life of the Christian Church."

It was a wonderful wedding. Three of our children sang "The Wedding Song" in the hall, and Canon Jim said he had "never known a wedding with such a 'lift' to it, a true Holy Spirit wedding."

The following morning when we woke together as husband and wife, sitting up in bed we asked the Lord for a scripture and His blessing on our union, and opened the Bible at Ephesians 5:21-25:

"Submitting to one another in the fear of God.

Wives, submit to your own husbands, as to the Lord.

For the husband is head of the wife, as also Christ is head of the Church; and He is the Saviour of the body.

Therefore, just as the Church is subject to Christ, so let the wives be to their own husbands in everything.

Husbands, love your wives, just as Christ also loved the Church and gave Himself for it……"

Thankyou Jesus for Your seal upon our marriage. We worked in the office all day and into the night as we were leaving the following day for a round-the-world honeymoon. The Lord had shown us some weeks before that we would arrive in Israel on either the 8th or 9th of November. We were scheduled to arrive on the 8th, but due to problems with the Airline were a day late, and arrived on the 9th, even as the Lord told us of the mix-up in advance.

## a) Honeymoon

We spent the first night in Israel at Mt. Tabor, from which Deborah and Barak swept down and defeated Sisera, where also Saladin, the leader of the Saracens set up his fort when fighting the Crusaders. We broke bread on the shores of the Sea of Galilee, and like the pilgrims of old read the "Psalms of Ascent" as we drove up to Jerusalem. We felt we were sharing our honeymoon with Jesus, His presence really close.

## b) Upper Room Anointing

I went through an amazing experience in the "Upper Room", a similar type of room to that in which the Last Supper was eaten, if not the room itself. I was walking around the room with perhaps sixty or seventy other tourists, when the Holy Spirit said quite plainly "Kneel down". "What, here Lord, in the middle of the room? I can't, all these people will think I'm crazy". "Kneel down", so I knelt, and began to weep and weep. Doug and Alan Alcock, our leader, saw me, came over and placed their hands on my head. All I could say was "Be it unto me according to Your Word", which was what Mary said when Gabriel told her she would have a baby, the Son of God.

Alan had a Word of Knowledge from the Holy Spirit and said "Do you know what that was all about?" as I stopped weeping. "No". "I believe the Lord will take you through a Gethsemane experience when you return home, a time of testing and loneliness, He is anointing you for it now." Thankyou Lord. Little did I know what was in store for me when we arrived home, but You knew Lord, and strengthened me for it.

Our ten days in Israel sped by and on the final evening we gathered for a farewell meeting. Eugene, a Roman Catholic Priest and Archaeologist spoke and brought a Prophecy. He said:

"I've been thinking of Ruth all day, and her recent marriage. This applies to us all really. Jesus is saying:

'What would you say if My face was disfigured?

'What would you say if you found that My face was the face of every poor man?

'What would you say if My face was the face of every person in this room?

'What would you say if you found that I had a wart on the chin, if My face was grubby and grey and My hair dishevelled?

'Would you find Me in your own self?

'My children, learn that My face is a human face, and that I do not come to you in a kind of aura of mystic power, but I come to you in a human, pysical and real way, and I want you to embrace Me in a human way, to receive Me in your way. Let Me take you in a human way. I want you to open yourself up as a bride greeting the bridegroom'."

Eugene said "I will never forget the days of the honeymoon with Jesus when I first gave my life to Him. He gave me this song:

"I will run in the Lord and dance in the Lord and
sing a melody.
I will run in the Lord and dance in the Lord and
sing a melody.
Sing, sing, sing in the Lord
Dance, dance, dance in the Lord
Arise My love, My fair one and come away,
Winter is past and dark is gone away.
I will make you My bride, so come away with Me,
Come away, come away, come away."

He loves us so much. This is a great mystery, but
we are actually betrothed to Him, and as such He
desires a warm close relationship with us.

Doug and I travelled home via Great Britain and
the States. I was very uneasy on the crossing between
Los Angeles and Honolulu, oppressed thinking of
Bob's death, quite resigned to death myself if this was
God's will, (which it obviously was not). Doug
accused me of being superstitious, and rightly discerned an attack of the devil. Praise God, I slept as we
passed the "point of no return", the place of Bob's
crash, and since then I've flown over the spot three
times and felt no fear. I was healed during this flight
with my new husband.

Margie and I moved into Doug's home at Longueville.

# Chapter 16
# **Prophecy Fulfilled**

After rearing a family at Lindfield for nineteen years, making all the decisions, acting father and mother and receiving complete co-operation from my children, I experienced quite a shock on arrival at my new home. Almost as soon as we arrived, Doug received the offer of a job as specialist Engineer at the Bougainville Copper Mines, New Guinea. The job was to take three months, and we agreed it was good he should go. He thus left me to settle in to the house with Margie and his three teenage daughters.

I soon found that the three Spencer girls were used to making their own decisions, and resented my intrusion, leaving me feeling a little like Elizabeth Elliot. She was led in to the Auca Indian Camp with her daughter. In fact, the Lord gave me exactly the same scripture He gave her, from Psalm 108:10:

"Who shall bring me into the strong city?"

The answer of course is the Lord.

Things were strained. Naturally it was difficult for Doug's girls to accept me, I was taking the place in their home of the mother they loved and missed. To be quite frank, I felt like going back to Lindfield many times, but my love for Doug, and the knowledge that I was in the centre of God's will kept me hanging in there. Another reason I had to stay was that the Crisis Call extension line was now connected to Longueville.

January, February passed, and then March, and Easter time. On Good Friday I was almost at rock bottom emotionally, and Saturday was probably worse. On Sunday morning Margie came in to me early and said "Mum, I've just had a vision, the first real one I've ever had. As I woke up I saw a beautiful cup, a gold communion cup, with jewels, a ruby, a sapphire, and an emerald. The cup was shrouded in mist, and suddenly a shaft of light shot from the cup and hit me in the chest. It was most precious."

I praised God for this, knelt down to talk to Him, and looked up at the bookcase. My eyes fell on a book called "Angels" by Billy Graham, and the Lord said to my spirit "Margie is your ministering angel. This loneliness and anguish you have been going through is what I told you about in Jerusalem, the Gethsemane experience. Jesus in the garden was alone and stricken, and longed that the cup should pass from Him, and then the angel came and ministered to Him.

This is your Gethsemane experience, and Margie, your angel, has just ministered to you."

I then remembered that it was Easter time again, as it was for Jesus. Praise God, I went down into darkness, but I came up into light, victorious.

Conditions at home improved greatly, especially as Doug arrived home soon after. My relationship now with Naomi, Liz and Susie is good, I love them, and I believe they love me. I realise I could never take their mother's place, and have never attempted to, but we are good friends, and I think we understand one another.

# Chapter 17
# Healing (Slipped Disc)

Many are subject to back trouble, and I was no exception. Born with a slight curvature of the spine, I didn't have any real trouble till Lindsay, my first child, was about twelve months old, and heavy to carry. From that time periodically I had a "bad back", occasionally confined to bed.

Early in the Christian walk I would pray about it and the Lord always healed, sometimes by rest, sometimes during the night when I was relaxed and the disc would slip almost audibly into place, a manipulation by the Lord.

Once or twice I felt led to call the doctor, and was given a course of Indocid to relax the spinal muscles. Once, when the disc was out of alignment, Margaret pushed me on the hip, manipulating it, as I have already written. Once I was chasing James to smack him, skidded on the polished floor, and when I picked myself up found my back completely healed.

This time I twisted suddenly picking up something heavy, and the pain was really acute. I lay flat in bed for five days, but was no better, experiencing great pain when I moved. There was a Full Gospel Businessmen's breakfast at Epping on the Saturday morning, and Doug encouraged me to attend because there would be healing prayer following the breakfast. He lowered the passenger seat in the car, and I lay supine all the way to Epping, Doug driving very carefully.

Two of the men helped me from the car. I needed prayer to enable me to sit through the meal, standing or lying down weren't too uncomfortable, but sitting was highly painful. After the meeting, Bill and David laid hands on my back and prayed for a healing. I could feel the power of the Holy Spirit pulsating into my back. When they said "Now touch your toes", the thought filled me with apprehension, but I raised my arms, swept forward and touched my toes by faith, and found I was healed! No pain, instant healing!

The healing was so complete, Doug and I did the week's shopping at the Supermarket on the way home. Afterwards we went down to the office and caught up on three hours typing and clerical work I'd been unable to do that week. Thank God!

# Chapter 18
# A New Church

A new Church had begun in Sydney, Christian
Life Centre. Doug and I were present at the first
meeting in a hall at Double Bay (there were twenty
five present, but now the church is the largest in
Sydney with a congregation of approximately three
thousand, and approximately two thousand in sub-
sidiary churches).

Pastor Frank Houston, in Lower Hutt, New Zealand, received a vision from the Lord which lasted
before his eyes for twelve hours. He could clearly see
the Sydney Harbour Bridge, Opera House and a large
black cloud over the Eastern Suburbs. The Lord gave
him a message from Isaiah 54:2:

"Lengthen your cords, and strengthen your
stakes".

He told Pastor Houston to leave his flourishing
church and Bible School, at Lower Hutt, and some of
his family, including children and grandchildren. He
was to begin a church in Sydney's Eastern Suburbs.

At that time there was no Pentecostal Church in the
Eastern Suburbs. All attempts to start one had failed,
but this was the Lord's time. "God's work, done at
God's time in God's way will never lack God's
supply, and will never fail."

## a) Wave of Revival

We were asked to fast and pray for an outpouring
of God's blessing in Sydney. Doug and I were at
Crisis Call praying with the duty counsellor before she

went on her telephone shift, when suddenly I saw something amazing.

I saw a beach, Bondi Beach, while my eyes were closed in prayer. A big blue wave, about twelve feet in height, was about to break right along the shore. It was a beautiful wave, there was no fear attached to the sight, but it was about to break on my head. Even though we were in the office, it was so real that I ducked! The wave was curling over at the top, with just a little white froth. Like Mary, I pondered in my heart what this could mean, and prayed asking the Lord for the interpretation.

I knew we were praying for blessing to roll in to Sydney through the Eastern Suburbs. Rev. Alan Langstaff had organised cars to travel backwards and forwards across Sydney with Christians praying in the Spirit, in tongues, taking the city for the Lord.

Alan's church at that time was "The Church in the Market Place", Bondi Junction. We went to this church to a service, Alan Langstaff preaching. To my amazement and delight I found in the square outside the church a mosaic of a tall blue wave with white froth on the curving top, just as I had seen it in my vision.

Alan was speaking of revival in Sydney and waves of blessing. That was in 1977. Blessing was sweeping into Sydney through the Eastern suburbs, and still is.

Alan Langstaff, on a visit from USA, spoke at Christian Life Centre, Darlinghurst this year, '86 about "Catching the Wave". We must be at the right place at the right time to catch a wave, and ride it. We must be expectant and alert and committed, otherwise we can be at the right place at the right time, and still not ready or recognise the right wave when it comes. Let us concentrate on catching God's Revival Wave. Alan had no idea I was in the congregation, or what a 'wave' meant to me. It was the Holy Spirit encouraging me to pray for the Wave of Revival.

## b) Crisis Call Handed Over

The Inaugural Meeting of Crisis Call was held on 10/6/78, exactly four years after it began as a service to the public. I woke with the word "Samuel", and realised that the Lord was speaking to me about Hannah in the first book of Samuel. She said "Lord, if you give me a baby boy, I will hand him back to You to serve You all the days of his life."

I, virtually the mother of Crisis Call, was handing it over to the Board to manage, in the name of the Lord. Ruth 4:15:

"And may he be to you a restorer of life and a nourisher of your old age".

Ruth also gave her baby to Naomi (representing the church) to nourish. Indeed Crisis Call is a full-time ministry for Doug and me to care for at a time in our lives when many people are considering retirement.

In other words, it's keeping us young.

# Chapter 19
# More Blessings

## a) U.S.A. Trip

Doug felt the Lord was calling us to attend an FBGMFI Convention (Full Gospel Businessmen's Fellowship International), in Anaheim, Calif., and travel on for business he had in New Jersey. He was praying at his desk first thing one morning "Lord, I've got so much work to finish here in Sydney - two large Specifications to get out - we will have to call off the trip." He opened his eyes and was looking at the cover of a "Voice" Magazine displaying in large print "Move it". "OK Lord, with Your help we can move it."

There was a tremendous amount of typing, (I was the typist), and so much copying, and we didn't own a copier at this stage. The Lord sent a salesman from ....Copiers, who insisted on leaving a copier with us for two days trial, with four reams of paper. We could copy as much as we wanted. We did. God is good to His own! This has never happened before or since. It saved us so much time doing the printing "in house".

So we 'moved' the load, and Margie came with us on the trip. Being prayed for before we left, someone had a "Word of Knowledge" that there would be "Fear on the plane". As we flew between Honolulu and Los Angeles, almost over the 'Point of no return' where Bob died, the Lord spoke to each of us three simultaneously to intercede in tongues. Minutes later we became aware that we were all interceding. Then up came the sign "Fasten seat belts".

Twenty minutes later we shared with one another how the Lord was calling us to pray, which we did silently. Doug prayed for the Captain, that he would be given the right decisions. I prayed for the salvation of the passengers. Doug, reading Proverbs, was given "Little did he know that his life was in danger."

I looked up at the film being shown to see the words "The End." We kept praying in the Spirit and gradually the situation cleared, the remainder of the flight uneventful. God only knows what our intercession prevented.

We had a wonderful holiday in the States, including the Convention in Anaheim, and a business trip to New Jersey and New York. We rubbed the moon rock in the Smithsonian Institute in Washington and visited friends in Gaithersburg, Maryland. We marvelled at the Oral Roberts University and the City of Faith, under construction, at Tulsa, Oaklahoma, and returned home via Oakland and San Fransisco.

## b) Lost Luggage

I had foolishly thought that in the few days leisure I might have time to begin writing this book, and took twenty years spiritual diary notes with me. Of course I didn't have a moment to look at the notes, but the devil struck a master blow! The suitcase containing the diary was missing when we returned to Sydney! "My God, help! If I don't have those notes there is no way I can write my book" He gave me Isaiah 56:1:

"Thus says the Lord: 'Keep justice, and do righteousness, for My salvation is about to come and My righteousness to be revealed'."

Also Isaiah 59:1:

"Behold, the Lord's hand is not shortened, that it cannot save."

I knew it would be returned. Margie prayed for a special angel to guard the case. During the night the cat jumped up on our bed, and carrying her outside in the dark, I stubbed my toe on our other suitcase still standing in the hall. I got back to bed, rubbing my toe, but the Lord said, "I want you to get up and pray for the return of the case."

There was a wonderful joy of the Lord's presence, and my faith was strengthened. I remembered King Jehoikim, who threw Jeremiah's scroll into the fire thinking he was destroying it, God spoke to Jeremiah and said "Go and write those words again, and more besides". Satan, you think you'll prevent me writing this book, but I tell you the Lord will give me the words, and bring to my remembrance all that is necessary to write. And anyway, I believe it is being guarded by an angel and will be returned."

Four days later United Airlines rang to say the missing case was standing with unclaimed luggage at Chicago! We'd not been anywhere near Chicago! Within two or three days Qantas phoned "We have a suitcase here from United Airlines for you."

## c) Counselling

A lady came to us at Crisis Call with many problems, and received the Lord Jesus into her life. She left full of the joy of the Lord, her mind now clear. One of the amusing things about this case was that a male boarder had moved out, owing rent, but leaving a double bed and wardrobe, using up space. She couldn't throw them out or sell them because they didn't belong to her. Then someone had a brilliant idea. Deliver them to his business office. She did. We laughed to think of his face when the furniture arrived.

A few days later the lady felt so good she brought her little girl in to hear about Jesus, (she had a stealing problem amongst other nasty habits).

I had had a strange dream the night before. The dream was about a little girl who came in for counselling, which I gave her, but didn't mention Jesus. When she was about to leave the plaque on the wall called out, "This child needs salvation", and I was ashamed at having to be reminded of such a thing.

I realised when I saw Emma that she was the girl of my dream. She handed her heart to Jesus, and not only was a changed person, but had not had a recurrence of the stealing problem when I spoke to her mother many months later.

## d) Healing (Knees)

I had had problems with my knees, first the left, then after that was healed, the right. I believe it was cartilege trouble, although I'm not sure because I felt led to approach the Lord for healing rather than the doctor. After dancing in the Spirit at Church my knee ached for days. It also troubled me if I walked up and down too many stairs. My left knee cracked and clunked and made incredible noises, and was extremely painful, even causing me to rest in bed on a couple of occasions.

Norman Armstrong was ministering healing at a meeting, and I joined the healing line. I told him my problem "When I dance in the Spirit my knee aches the following day." Norman laid his hands on my head and said "This will never happen again. Be healed in Jesus' name, and you will dance before the Lord." I was instantly healed.

About two years later the other knee began to ache. I recorded in my diary "Knee very painful, so painful the cracks and thumps it gives drain me of all my energy, almost like an electrical discharge or loss. It is just tiring me out."

At this time we used to attend the Fellowship meeting at Epping, (FGBMFI), and a friend, John, while talking to the Lord in the morning was told by Him "A lady who is falling with pain will be at the meeting tonight. If you lay hands on her and she will be healed." I had fallen with the pain that morning, clutching at the table for support.

During the meeting, conducted by Bill, John stood and announced that there was a lady, falling with pain in her knee, and that if she came forward for prayer the Lord would heal her. I jumped up saying "It's me". John laid hands on my head, prayed for healing and said "You will dance before the Lord", exactly the same words spoken over me two years previously, but by another person. I knew I was healed. Within a week there was not a twinge of pain in either knee. That was eight years ago, and I've had no pain or problems since.

# Chapter 20
# God Speaks At Goulburn

Intercession! Spiritual warfare! Three weeks instruction on seeking God, speaking to Him, hearing from him, waiting on Him! Altered lives - Altared lives! Committment! Death to self! Missionary Commission!

How do we disentangle ourselves from all our committments and responsibilities for three whole weeks? Who will look after Crisis Call and Doug's work?

"When God calls He enables". He of course provided, and Doug, James (our son), and I, found ourselves with over seventy other leaders at this wonderful seminar, the camp of a lifetime!

It began quietly enough. The usual introductions, "getting to know you", getting to know Tom Hallis and other leaders from YWAM (Youth With A Mission), in whose premises we were housed, and in conjunction with whom Intercessors for Australia were conducting the Camp.

Dean Sherman gave the first week's instruction, Loren Cunningham (founder of YWAM) the second and then Joy Dawson brought the challenge to action in the final week. In between teaching sessions Noel Bell led the intercession. All was enjoyable and serene.

Suddenly at the beginning of the second week the scene changed.

There had been many prophecies, but now, through an Archdeacon:

"I am coming to you as a flensing knife to pare

away that which had sheltered you, to change it in form, to render it down that it might become the oil of usefulness to Me."

Silence.

What is a "flensing knife"? The Archdeacon who gave the prophecy had never heard of a "flensing knife". This in itself was a thrill and encouragement to me. It proves once again that in true prophecy the words given are from the Lord, because the man didn't know exactly what he was saying, just obediently bringing the words given by the Holy Spirit.

Doug was the only one present who knew what a "flensing knife" was, following an engineering job on a whaling station. The prophecy was a metaphor taken from "Whaling". A flensing knife is a large blunt wedge knife which forces apart the covering blubber and the flesh beneath, a gentle action, no cutting. He explained that in whaling the blubber is rendered or boiled down to produce the precious whale oil so much sought after in days gone by.

So God was saying "I am coming to take away the thick layer under which you are sheltering, to expose you and set you free so that what used to be your covering will be changed into something useful to Me."

From that moment all "Heaven" broke loose.

Such a time of exposure, as our masks and coverings were removed. This was done gently (like flensing), as each one was constrained, almost compelled, by the Holy Spirit to confess his (or her) sins, and lay his inner life open to the assembled gathering. It was an obedience, a voluntary exposure.

As each one opened himself/herself to the others, before the Lord, great compassion and love was extended to them, and a wonderful relief and joy to those

150

who were exposed and healed and filled with the Holy Spirit. This move of the Spirit extended over one week till most people present had been moved upon to throw themselves on God's mercy, and that of the assembled saints.

What a oneness this forged between us! What a relief to know that others too had experienced suppressed guilts and fears. One of Satan's greatest lies is "If people only knew what you are really like they would reject you." In fact, the opposite is the case. When we see others as vulnerable as we are, we love them for it and our Christian bond grows stronger.

As Noel Bell, the leader said, "What began as a Camp in Intercession has become a Camp in Humility."

Repentant and thankful and broken before Jesus, we were now ready for "the challenge" of the third week. Joy Dawson brought this challenge.

It began in an unexpected way. We were all waiting eagerly for Joy's arrival, agog with excitement. The evening meeting began at 8pm, and by 7.30 people were arriving with rugs and blankets and bibles. By 8 o'clock the room was full.

8.15 came, 8.30, 8.45 - no Joy Dawson.

At 9pm she sent a message, "I have nothing to say".

Great disappointment at first, but we talked to Jesus and said "We didn't come here to hear Joy Dawson, we really came to hear from you", and repented.

It reminded us of the time when YWAM was reaching out to buy a ship "The Agape", in which to carry the Gospel around the world, when the Holy Spirit brought a vision to Loren. Everyone was standing looking at the ship, with their whole attention towards it, and their backs to Jesus.

Jesus said "Give the money you have received for the "Agape" to ..... who were then buying their second Missionary ship. Everyone was aghast, but repentant, and in obedience gave the money as Jesus directed. He is so faithful, and later gave them a larger ship "The Anastassius", meaning "The Resurrection". (It had been death to their plans, but the Lord resurrected them.) Praise God.

We were looking to Joy Dawson's arrival, and had turned our backs on the Lord. At 9.15pm we were in the swing of a great prayer meeting when Joy arrived. I for one was almost disappointed to see her. She explained at first that she was only the donkey on which the Lord was riding, and then gave the message, which she had received as soon as we repented.

The challenge she gave later that week, and our response, is written in the next chapter.

# Chapter 21
# Our Mission to Moscow

(I wrote the following article in 1980 on our excursion through the USSR via the Trans Siberian Railway. It was never submitted for publication, and although written seven years ago, still covers an important adventure in our lives.)

## Our Mission to Moscow

### a) The Vision

"And it shall come to pass afterward that I will pour out My Spirit on all flesh; your sons and your daughters shall prophesy, your old men shall dream dreams, your young men shall see visions;
And also on My menservants and on My maidservants I will pour out My Spirit in those days."
Joel 28, 29. (Acts 2:17, 18)

Perhaps Joel and Peter couldn't envisage women seeing visions, but praise God they do!

Doug and I were with approximately seventy Church and Christian group leaders at a three week seminar on Intercession. In the second week the prayers began focusing on Russia and the Iron Curtain countries.

The Lord wonderfully revealed aspects of the powers of darkness over the USSR. We groaned in the Spirit as we saw, through prophecy and words of knowledge, the bondage of the Soviet people.

We were shown that the Lord wanted some to visit

this land and show love and joy to the people, and be witnesses for Him. We prayed for 100 apostles of love and joy to go to Russia. We also prayed that our attitudes be released from fear and prejudice so that we could see the Russians as He sees them. We remembered the occasion in January '78 when Alan Langstaff was proclaiming "A New Day" on the Opera House steps. A passing Russian ship tooted loudly - many thought it sounded like an 'Amen.'

We laid hands on the map of the USSR and projected joy and love to the people.

One week later Joy Dawson said "I feel God will do dynamic things in this room. Let us offer a huge prayer request, a creative thing, a big prayer that will further His work in the world." Then after a short silence, she said "I feel a vision is now being released."

At this moment I received the vision that God used to send us to the USSR.

Standing with eyes closed I realised that half the screen of my vision as dark and half light. Examining the outline closely, I realised I was looking at the coast of Siberia. When I recognised that, the scene changed, and I saw a heavy mist, and then a strange grey-white ship, about four decks in height, but small and old-fashioned, unlike any ship I had ever seen before. The ship faded, a train hooted loudly down at the station, then as clearly as anything on a TV screen, I could see a large metal bowl high on the left of my eyes, containing the Olympic Flame. The message was unmistakable, we were to go to Russia, at the time of the Olympic Games. By train and ship?

A further verification of the call to Russia came later the same day. The Dean of Goulburn offered to show a group over the Cathedral. When he finished, he took us to the safe and said "Wait till you see what I have here." He produced a most beautiful Russian Cross in silver, bejewelled with amethysts. A Russian Orthodox Priest had donated it to the Cathedral. It was a large cross, about four inches in length, a most unlikely thing to be found in a safe in an Australian country town.

I asked if I could hold the cross, and as I did a real surge of love for the Russian people overwhelmed me, and a longing to go to the USSR was birthed in my spirit.

Those of us who received the call to Russia felt the Lord was saying "Would you be prepared to go to prison for Me in the USSR?' Ghastly thought, but we all said "Yes, Lord'. "Would you go to a Psychiatric Hospital for Me in the USSR?" Groans! "Yes, Lord."

One year later every aspect of the vision came to pass, and we were tested once again about going to prison for Jesus' sake when we entered USSR. Praise God, we didn't have to go to prison, but the possibility has left us with a burning desire to reach out to our brothers and sisters in Communist prisons.

## b) The Preparation

Eight months after the Intercessors Seminar, about forty Christians called by the Lord to visit the USSR met together. With us were Russian-born Christians who spoke the language fluently, and others who were to instruct us about reaching out to the Russian people.

As we met for prayer, a prophecy was given with the theme "You do the possible, and God will do the impossible."

Our outreach was typified by an escapade described in 1 Samuel 14:1-23. The Philistines were grouped in large numbers preparing for confrontation with Israel. Jonathan and his armour bearer climbed up and engaged the Philistines in combat. In spite of the seemingly impossible situation, the two men, with God, began the routing of the Philistine Army.

The situation typified our little band moving into the land of the USSR, which is armed against Christianity. We are inclined to hide in the rocks as Christians, like the Israelites, and say "What can we do? We are so few and they are so many. How can we go into their territory? We'll be annihilated. We don't have the language, what is the use if we can't converse? It can't be done!"

Consider the power of Communist Russia. The Communists are on the offensive; they are building a political system which is becoming a religion. They must resist Christianity and keep it out of the country. It is a threat to their whole existence.

Communism is the religion they are building, Lenin is the god.

We considered the fact that there has never been a greater enemy to the Church than Communism. Its goal is the annihilation of the Church. There have been more Christians put to death in our day than in all the preceding centuries of Christianity.

Since World War 2, many countries have fallen to Communism, but where are the Christians? Hiding in the rocks like Israel before the Philistines. We must present ourselves to them, stand up and be counted.

Jesus said "All authority is given unto Me ......therefore GO." Matt 28:18, 19. We don't have to ask any country's permission, but we must not be hung up about breaking the law of the land when preaching the Gospel either at home or abroad. We belong to another kingdom, and we have Jesus' command "Go!"

Paul says in Romans 13:1 "Submit to the governing authorities," but where did Paul spend most of his time? In gaol, in escapes, in hiding, in building up the underground Church.

Peter wrote "Submit yourselves to every ordinance of man for the Lord's sake," 1 Pet 2:13. The latter end of that verse shows that this authority is limited to punishing evildoers and praising those who do right. If I do wrong, I need to fear authority, but if I do right, there is nothing to fear.

Peter himself was thrown into gaol, but rescued by an angel. He said "We need to obey God rather than man." Acts 4:19.

We work within the framework of the law of the land if necessary to help change the wrong laws. We need to do this in our own country as well as others.

## The law of God says

Thou shalt love the Lord thy God
Teach all men
Repent and be baptised
Teach children to love and know God

## The law of the USSR says

Love the State, there is no God
No evangelism
No baptism
No Christian instruction of children

Joining the Communist Youth Movement at 14, 15 corresponds to our Confirmation ........perhaps!
There is separation of Church and State in the USSR - to put the Church down.
In the USA - to permit the Church to flourish? It is

now used to take prayer out of schools, parliament etc.
In Australia - following USA pattern.
In Britian - no separation yet.

We realised that even if we were caught with Bibles there must be no lying or dishonesty of any kind. We just always tell the truth even if we risk being sent out of the country. We must be careful not to slip into "Situational Ethics," eg. the end justifies the means, everything is alright if done in love. There is no end to this downward slide.

Like Jonathan and his armour bearer we were to make our presence known. It was said of Paul and Silas "They cause trouble all over the world" Acts 17:6. Let's stir for Jesus sake, and let everyone know we are there. But remember to stay away from politics. We are there representing another kingdom, there to talk about Jesus.

## Soviet Legalities

We were shown how we would stand legally if apprehended, and were to familiarise ourselves with the following rules:

Declaration of Human Rights - U.N. Membership

Article 18 - Freedom of thought, conscience and religion

Article 19 - Freedom of opinion and expression.
"Lenin, Complete Collective Works" Vol 7.
Everyone must have complete freedom of faith to

(a) hold
(b) propogate
(c) change

their beliefs. There must be freedom of assembly, speech etc. "to strengthen the Soviet System."

It was shown us that the Word of God in principle strengthens the Civil System. Big problems are alcoholism, working absenteeism, minimum work (go slow), covering up, subterfuge, lying, black market, taking of bribes.

A few weeks later I read in "Time" Magazine, June 23, 1980, p55 an article headed "A Bit Wild in the Big City." Subheading "Youth crime grows, as booze spreads and Babushka recedes' (The Babushka is the Grandmother who used to help rear and control the children, also take them to Church).

The article tells of youth crime, cruelty, violence, theft, murder and hooliganism in Moscow. Quote "It is not only the extent of juvenile crime that worries the Soviets, but the ideological contradiction that is involved. In a Communist Society antisocial behaviour should be on the wane. It hits the regime where it hurts most."

We were told to keep a positive outlook towards the State as such, and loyal up to the point where they won't allow us to be Christians. We were to try to show friendship, love and joy to the Russian people.

We were told to love the KGB agents. Minister to them, not to be secretive, but to reveal ourselves to them. Show them what Christians are like. We laughed, and agreed to go on a "KGB Ministry." If we had to fill in reports, we decided to make them a witness to the people who would read them. "My name will bring you before authorities, rulers, courts, and you will witness for Me," Jesus said.

The population of the USSR in 1980 was 262,400,000, composed of 100 different nations, speaking over 100 different languages. They all have their own Governments, but are controlled by Moscow.

The Tsarist rule and its feudal system ended in

1917 when Tsar Nicholas was shot. Russia was set back by World War 1, then the Revolution, then World War 2. She trailed 50-100 years behind the Western World in '80, but perhaps the gap is closing.

In the 1930's, Stalin, establishing the Industrialization Revolution, and Collectivism, used purges and starvation to get results. Life is better now, more freedom, less hardship.

## Philosophy of Communism

We were taught, very briefly and simply, that this is partly based on the teachings of Emmanual Kant, on cause and effect, doing your own thing. Whatever seems good to you is truth. However, Dialectical Materialism is the main basis of Communism as taught by Huegel and Feyerbach. Two truths clash, spawn and form a new truth, and by this means we advance. There is no need for God.

Darwin's teaching says there is no absolute beginning, man evolved, is matter in motion. Freud says, because there is no God, there are no absolutes for morality, and there is no reason for guilt. Do your own thing and be free from guilt.

Karl Marx said "The property class used religion as the opiate of the people. Give them religion, and it'll take their mind off the problem."

Lenin said "We will destroy everything, and on the ruins build our temple."

## Selfishness undercuts Communism

If Communism could have come by education they would have it by now, after seventy years attempt. After revolution, then counter-revolution, the situation is reverting back to what it was before - selfish ness, with the "elite", the heads of Government, earning high salaries, owning expensive cars, holiday homes on the Black Sea etc., while the workers are poor and oppressed.

President Tito of Yugoslavia said to Eleanor Roosevelt, "There will never be Communism until we can remove selfishness from the heart of men."

## The Socialist State

The perfect example of the Socialist State is the Bee Hive. The Hive is everything. All is for the good of the Hive. Everybody works. Everyone's needs are met. Step out of line and you are rejected. There is no creativity, no place for individualism, no place for the old and infirm non-workers. In the State they are institutionalised (beware Euthanasia and Abortion), and in the Hive they are destroyed. There is an elite society of "drones" who do very little but wait on the Queen.

Man is just a clever animal in the Communist System. Because there is no God, and no absolutes, man degenerates morally. He becomes selfish, lazy, cold, without love. The Communist Art is cold and lifeless, industrialised Art.

President Tito was one of the world's richest men. The Russian leaders are wealthy. Is this a classless society? There is always a reversion to selfishness.

We were challenged. The world is waiting for the answer, while here we sit. We must bring the world back to absolutes, God, His Word, the Bible. We have the answers, we need to go. We need to tell people so that they may make a clean choice to accept God or reject Him.

The Lord is sending the Gospel into the USSR today.

Lenin said just before he died, "With ten men like St. Francis of Assisi we could have won the World".

There was to be a confrontation, a clash, a goal, an obedience to the command "Go into all the World and preach the Gospel to every creature."

Rom. 10:13-15:

"Whoever calls upon the name of the Lord shall be saved."

"How then shall they call on Him in whom they have not believed? And how shall they believe in Him of Whom they have not heard? And how shall they hear without a preacher? And how shall they preach unless they are sent? As it is written: 'How beautiful are the feet of those who preach the gospel of peace, who bring glad tidings of good things!'"

## c) The Provision

According to the vision given us by the Lord, we knew we must travel to Moscow via the Trans Siberian Railway. This was to cost $9,000.00 for Doug and me, including the rest of the trip. We had saved this amount, but had lent the money to a friend who guaranteed to repay it in time for us to buy the tickets. Our hearts sank when he informed us that the money was tied up, and he could not repay it. "Lord, You called us to go for You to the USSR, please provide the money," we prayed.

Then of course our wonderful Lord provided. A miraculously early payment of an Engineering Project in which Doug was engaged suddenly came to hand, and we were able to buy our tickets in time.

Another miraculous provision of money was made to our daughter and son-in-law, Margie and Roger, who were also travelling to Moscow, and were believing in faith for their fare. Out of the blue a letter arrived addressed to me from the Worker's Compensation advising me that an amount of over $30,000.00 was lying unclaimed in their Department. This money had been awarded me and my four children on the death of my first hushand, twenty two years previously. I had forgotten about it years ago. Did we need the money now? Did we ever! The cheque arrived on the very last day in April when they were due to pay their fare.

Doug and I rang them that night. "Do you have your money for Russia?" we asked. "Not yet", they replied in faith. "How much do you need?" They mentioned the amount. "The Lord sent the money in for you today, we'll post the cheque tomorrow." There was silence, and then two young people laughing and crying at the same time. Praise God. The Lord raised our faith level by His miracles.

Doug and I needed one more major miracle. We are the Directors of a 24-hour emergency telephone counselling service in Sydney. This had to be provided for not only by Counsellors to man the phones day and night, but we also needed a couple to live in our house and supervise the work, taking responsibility for decision making, face-to-face counselling etc.

We prayed for this couple for months, but still no-one suitable was found. We paid our fares in faith, knowing that without the right people to help, we simply couldn't go. We also knew by faith that the Lord would send the special ones He had chosen, for when God calls, He enables:

In the very last week, the Lord sent to us a New

Zealand Pastor and his wife, on four months evangelical itinerary. They were able to supervise the work for six weeks until Roger and Margie arrived back from the USSR, who then took over for the next four weeks until we arrived home. Thank God.

## d) The Journey Begins

At a service four nights before our journey began, Doug and I received the laying-on-of-hands. Prayers were offered for our safety, travelling mercies, and the success of our mission. We were given the message from a hymn:

"You will speak your words to foreign men,
And they will understand.
Be not afraid, I go before you always,
Come follow Me, and I will give you rest."

Janet Hemans.

We do appreciate and love all our Christian friends. What a comfort to know that there is someone loving and praying back home, and what a difference it makes to the situation!

We were thankful too, for the prayers of our Church group on Sunday morning before we left. The Lord gave us a prophecy in which He said:

"You have sought My face in these matters, and I am with you, and I will guide you. I will grant you the opening of the mouth and understanding of the Spirit. You shall go out in the comfort and Spirit of God. The wisdom of man faileth, but the wisdom of God faileth not. There shall not be a hastiness of spirit in you. God will bless you and others will be converted because of you, and you'll meet them in Heaven".

The words of this prophecy came to pass in the

USSR, and when we get to Heaven we expect to see the rest fulfilled.

A child stood and read a passage from Isaiah 61:1-7. She was unaware that this is a vital message for us, and we took this as a further verification of our mission.

In order to avoid confusion, I shall list the countries we visited in order of arrival, on the first stage of our trip.

| | |
|---|---|
| New Zealand (Auckland) | 1 week |
| Honolulu | 2 days |
| Japan | 2 days |
| USSR | 16 days |
| Scandanavia | 6 days |

Doug and I left Sydney for New Zealand on June 29, 1980, on the first leg of our journey. On arrival in Auckland we met the other members of the Christian group with whom we would be travelling. In the week of waiting we prayed together, shared and got to know each other.

As we all prayed together one morning, I saw the picture of a train, travelling in the dark, just before dawn. I was in the driver's cabin and could see the headlights of the train as it thundered along, showing up the tracks as they stretched straight ahead into the darkness. The trees and hills were still black, but the clouds ahead were a rosy pink, and the Spirit said "That is the light of a New Day, a New Day is dawning in Russia".

This was also a fulfilment of Alan Langstaff's words "It's a New Day," on the steps of the Opera House at the commencement of the Jesus '78 Conference. Actually he was referring to Australia, but as he said these words, a passing Russian ship sounded its siren, as though Russia was included in this. To me she was. It is a new day of hope and joy for the Russian Church, praise God.

After one week together, the group had been welded into a united body, and was ready to launch out.

We left Auckland Airport on the 6th July, with a typical Christian farewell - guitars, singing, sharing with the interested bystanders. Relatives and friends gathered to bid us 'God speed'.

With a few words of witness to the small crowd gathered, our leader spoke of Jesus' love and explained that we were a Christian group about to travel the world telling people that Jesus loves them. By the time we had hugged everybody and gathered up our gear, there was hardly a dry eye. Praising God we moved through the barrier, and on to exciting new horizons.

## e) Honolulu

Good to see the magnificent, swaying coconut palms of Honolulu and smell the heavily perfumed frangipani leis around our necks once more. Wonderful to feel the warm, moisture laden trade winds after the cold wet winter conditions in New Zealand.

Reading his Bible as we came in to land, Doug saw the words "And the Holy Spirit came to rest on Him like a dove", just as we touched the runway. White doves or pigeons flew on to the balcony outside our room at the hotel as though to greet us. It seemed like a visit from the Holy Spirit Himself. We fed the birds with crumbs, which they ate out of our hands, and strutted cautiously into the room as we lured them in with more crumbs. Like the locals, they mainly live off the tourists.

"A swim, that's what we need," we said.

"Don't forget to witness," reminded our leader.

We jostled our way along the beach at Waikiki, and swam, praying for someone to witness to. The smell of coconut oil suntan lotion hung heavily in the air. Wealthy men and women, bulging and with obvious signs of great affluence, lazed on the beach, with bored expressions, unhappy in their perfect freedom. There seemed to be an air of disinterest everywhere, and I must admit we returned to our hotel discouraged, having spoken to no one.

Jesus' words "It is easier for a camel to pass through the eye of a needle than for a rich man to enter the kingdom of God," came to mind.

Honolulu must be one of the wealthiest parts of the world. Rich holiday makers relax here with every conceivable luxury. But money cannot buy happiness. I sometimes wonder how much money a millionaire would be prepared to pay if he could buy Jesus' joy. Jesus is the way, the only way. "Please Jesus, soften their hearts and open their eyes to see You and their need to be saved."

We had practiced street singing and witnessing on late shopping night in Auckland, a new experience for Doug and me, so when we began singing Christian songs in Honolulu on the sidewalk we were not quite so self conscious as we had been at first. However, we were not so well received in Honolulu.

By the comments of a few young people as they passed, like "What's the place coming to with all this religion? Why do they allow it?" etc., we sensed strong spiritual opposition. Very few passers-by showed any interest whatsoever, others stared with stony faces as they hurried past. The God of Mammon has a powerful stronghold in opulent Honolulu. Anyway, we enjoyed the witnessing even if they didn't, and we were able to talk to a few folk who stopped to listen.

"Come on team, no lazing around in Honolulu, we have an appointment with a train in the USSR.

All aboard the airport bus."

## f) Japan

Leaving Honolulu, we flew in to Narita Airport, Tokyo, and received a rude shock. Doug and I were arrested!

The New Zealanders have a reciprocal arrangement with Japan that neither need visas in the other's country. There were three of us with Australian Passports, and we were under the impression that visas were not necessary as we were only in the country less than 72 hours. How wrong we were!

The three of us were stopped by the Customs agents and marched down the corridor to a small room, where Japanese Immigration Officials scuttled in and out. We were informed that we were in Japan illegally as we had no visas, and would have to leave.

"What can we do?" we asked apprehensively. "You can ask for a Hearing of your case." "Very well, we should like to have a Hearing."

We sat while they prepared documents, conferrred in Japanese, adjourned to another room for the Hearing. Meanwhile the rest of our group was conveyed to their Tokyo Hotel.

Some time later the Japanese Officials returned, sat down opposite us behind a long desk, presented each of us with a typed document headed "Notice of Decision in Hearing." Underneath were the dreaded words, "You do not conform to the conditions for landing ..... as a valid visa is not affixed to your passport. If you do not agree to the decision you may file an objection against the Minister of Justice. When you agree to the decision, you shall be ordered to leave Japan."

"But we can't do that," we wailed, "we must cross the country tomorrow to catch the USSR Aeroflot plane at Niigata." (Niigata is on the west coast of Japan).

"No, you must leave the country. You may fly to Seoul, Korea, Hong Kong or back to Australia."

"No, no, no, you don't understand, we must catch the Russian plane, we are booked on the Trans Siberian Train which leaves in two days time."

"Very sorry. You must leave Japan."

"Yes, that's what we want to do - from Niigata."

"No. That is impossible. You cannot enter Japan. You must fly from this Airport. No planes from here fly to Niigata or USSR."

"What can we do?"

"You may appeal to the Minister of Justice. This takes at least three days."

"Very well, we appeal - please try to hurry the appeal - we must cross Japan tomorrow night at the latest."

We were then very cordially and politely bowed out and escorted to rooms in a luxurious Airport Hotel, with an armed guard clutching a walky-talky sitting outside the door. We were under house arrest.

During the night we could hear the guards conversing softly as they changed shifts. In the morning as we left our room for breakfast, the guard smiled and nodded politely, and informed the front desk that we had left our rooms and were entering the lift.

We were prisoners in the Hotel. We rested in our rooms, slept and waited all that day. We contacted the Australian Embassy, but they could do nothing. In the evening, in the nick of time word came through from the Minister of Justice that our appeal had been upheld, and we were granted permission to enter Japan and cross the country.

Praising God we grabbed our luggage and raced off to catch the overland train. We noticed that the guard had gone; their prisoners, Doug and I and a drug pusher, had been dealt with.

Now, with cries of "Look out Russia, here we come," we boarded the train, and looked around to see who we could witness to.

Little did we know that our brush with the law in Japan was nothing to what was ahead at the USSR border. With joy we crossed Japan and joined our group in Niigata.

## g) Incident at the Border

Who was the well-dressed man pacing up and down slowly at the Airport casting occasional glances towards us? Why was he looking at us so furtively, but searchingly, as though summing us up?

Our leader took me aside and spoke softly. "Ruth, take the Cross from around your neck, I suspect that man watching us is a KGB agent. He's probably seen it already."

As I quickly slipped the Cross into my pocket I held it lovingly for a moment. All those Bibles in Doug's case. "Please Lord, don't let them be found."

I remembered how we had packed that morning. When we were called, by Jesus, to go for Him to Russia, He had spoken so clearly to each of us individually, "Would you go to prison for Me in the USSR?" We had both said "Yes, Lord." But that was one year ago, and now we must face this question again.

We decided that it would be foolish both going to prison for smuggling Bibles, so Doug insisted we put them all in his case - I could go back home and hold the fort till Doug returned.

The Lord had shown Doug to take in nearly twenty Gospels of John (The Russians call any portions of the Scriptures 'Bibles'). He showed him to place three New Testaments in the side pocket of his brief case. These three were not discovered. Indeed, if we had been obedient and taken only those Scriptures shown us to take by the Lord, we would have been successful in getting them across the border.

Now we were faced with reality, approximately forty 'Bibles'. How to get them past the Border Guards?

We had been reading a book called "Mission Possible", in which the Christians crossing the border had prayed that the guards wouldn't see the suitcase, and they didn't. Could we believe for a miracle like this? Yes, why not!

Boarding Call, Aeroflot, Soviet bound.

There she stood, a small white jet, red flag, "CCCP" painted on her fusilage (SSSR in English), flying us from freedom into ......what?

Flying through much mist and cloud, (as seen in my vision at Goulburn), we touched down in Khabarovsk, USSR, Far Eastern Siberia. We taxied from the strip in amongst debris, dugouts, piles of building material, heaped earth, to the Airport Arrivals Building. There for the first time we saw the dominating 5-pointed star of USSR, representing the five continents of the world (yet to be liberated, our guide reluctantly admitted). It is the emblem of expansionist Communism, a challenging symbol to the Countries of the Iron Curtain, sinister to those not under its shadow.

The Airport Arrivals Building reminded one of a large imposing Manor House, with high decorated ceilings, large arched windows, pillars, the chapters of which bore the 5-pointed star, but the stylish atmosphere of the building was spoiled by the rough partitioning in it, and the dirty, untidy, makeshift atmosphere and confusion everywhere.

"Do you have any pornographic or religious literature?" My heart missed a beat.

"Yes, religious literature," said Doug. We had agreed that as Christians we must tell the truth at all times, even a lie to save Bibles was unthinkable. The Customs Official pointed to my case. "Please open," she said, and almost immediately found a pile of "Voice" magazines, written in French, German, Italian and Scandinavian languages.

"What are these books? Religious books?"

"Yes, but they are not in the Russian language, we are taking these through the country to Scandinavia."

She placed the magazines numbering about one hundred, on the table. Having examined the rest of the contents of my bag closely, she turned to Doug "Now your case," she said. "Oh no," my heart murmured, "Please Lord, don't let her see them."

The Customs official was so charming, softly spoken and feminine, I found it difficult to identify her with the grim-faced men of iron I had expected to encounter at the Border. She was pretty, gentle, all-woman, and I admired her greatly, but she kept digging mercilessly deeper and deeper into the suitcase.

With each handful she took out our hearts sank lower and lower. Silence. She called a male assistant. Together they transferred the Bibles to the table.

Eventually all our precious Bibles were stacked on the table, except the three New Testaments which the

Lord had shown Doug to hide in the pocket of the briefcase. Other Customs Officials were summoned, and two men carried the booty, whilst another said politely "Please come with us," and off we marched single file, through the terminal and down into a small room for questioning.

The officer in charge sat at the desk, the Bibles laid out before him. In the background stood the men who carried them. Doug and I were asked to be seated. Two interpreters were present, one of whom was the girl who found the books and tracts. The officer in charge called another policeman with a videotape camera unit, with which he proceeded to videotape the proceedings, including our faces no doubt, as we answered questions, and then Doug's personal papers.

Meanwhile, the other members of our group viewed our "arrest" with apprehension and dismay, but they were hastened through the Customs inspection, and although a few Bibles were intercepted no-one was detained.

I praised God in my heart that I had no fear, for He had taken that from me before I left Australia, in a marvellous way. If there had been any fear in me, it would have risen to overwhelm me now. I felt strangely cornered. Never having been apprehended by Police in my life, I began to realise how a law-breaker must feel when he is caught redhanded.

"Why have you brought these Bibles into the country?"

"We heard the Russian Christians want Bibles."

"But surely you must know what our rules are?"

"No."

"But surely you must know what our rules are?"

"I've always been puzzled about what your rules are."

"It's against the rules of our country."

"But we thought you had freedom of religion here."

Silence.

"If the Bible is such a dangerous book why did you print 30,000 Russian Bibles yourselves?"

Silence.

"Why did you bring the Bibles in?"

"The Bible means as much to Christians as Lenin's works mean to you, in fact even more," Doug explained.

I spluttered. Something told me we were getting on to dangerous ground here. I made some 'Oil on troubled waters' clucking noises.

The officer in charge gave an incredulous half-smile, and looked somewhat bewildered. However, he still insisted we couldn't bring these religious books into the USSR.

"You brought them in to give to Christians? Soviet citizens?"

We said many things which were not interpreted, because they were getting together trying to work out what they were going to ask us next.

"What are these Full Gospel Business Men's Books?"

Immediately wheeling the camera round, the Officer zeroed in on the magazines in question.

"They are not even in the Russian language, we are taking them through the country to Scandinavia. May we have them back?"

"No, there are too many of them."

"May we have the Bibles back?"

"No."

"Some of those books are my own personal reading," I said, "they are not to give away. May I have them please?"

The officer in charge nodded his head, and handed

back my books, plus our own English Bibles.

We were asked many more questions, quizzed closely as to our heritage - did any of our forebears come from Russia? Did we have any relatives or friends in the USSR? Did we know any Christians? Where were we intending to take the Bibles? To whom were we intending to give the Bibles? Then personal questions. What did Doug do to earn a living? What was his income? What did I do? How could Doug get time off to come to USSR if he was a working man? Did he have his own business? How often did we have holidays? How many children did we have? What were their ages? Where did we get the Bibles? What was our organisation?

By this time it was about 8pm, and everyone was tired. The officer in charge indicated that it was time to go home.

Doug and I were told that there was a bus outside waiting to take us to the Intourist Hotel where we were staying. We didn't realise how long we had been under interrogation, but over three and a half hours had passed since we were separated from our group.

On arrival at the Hotel we were shown our room, and then our Intourist guide escorted us to the dining room for a meal. We were both in a state of shock at this stage, and didn't really feel hungry.

Looking around the dining room we found the Russian people interesting and attractive. The large dining room had been turned into a sort of disco, with young people sitting at tables drinking vodka, and eating various things. The night was hot, being the middle of summer, and many young people were outside in the cool night air. Others were dancing. There are mosquitoes in USSR too, I noticed.

As we sat watching, we noticed one young man staggering across the room, tears pouring down his face. Someone produced a box of tissues. Then another boy, also crying. Then a third. "What emotional men they have in the USSR", I thought to myself. However, Doug and I were too tired and dispirited to care. We crossed the room to the foyer, when suddenly we were hit by a wave of irritating gas. Our eyes began to water and a choking sensation attacked our throats. Tear gas. Doug and I both served in the '39-'45 war, and the gas experience took us straight back to wartime training. What was tear gas doing in a Siberian Disco?

We stepped over a broken Vodka bottle on the floor by the lift and walked wearily to our room. Police were scurrying around. Such a thing had never happened before they said, but then there were foreigners in the Hotel.

Next morning I woke early and knelt beside my bed and prayed. "Lord Jesus, what will happen? Will they come back? Will they take us in for further questioning? Will they question us about the other members of the group? Will they realise that we are organised to take this country spiritually for You, our God? Will we go to prison? Is this what You foresaw when You asked would we be prepared to go to prison for You? Lord Jesus, what are we to do?"

I opened by Bible to read my portion for the day, and happened to open at the Book of Jeremiah, right at the verses Chap 38:6, "So they took Jeremiah and put him into a cistern (of a prison.)"

Lord God, we're going to prison!

I shared this with Doug, who was not surprised. He had been told twice by the Lord in the last two days that he was to go through a chastening experience, so we had to face this together before the Lord. We then packed Doug's case for prison. I put in it all the toothpaste, two bottles of vitamin pills, all the soap, towels, warm gear, and everything we had to make prison as bearable as possible.

We waited.

While we were waiting I looked carefully out of the window, and received a wonderful assurance from the Lord. The strange ship I had seen in my vision was anchored in the river not far from our hotel.

It was a shabby off-white colour, about four decks in height, and was a river boat with many portholes and cabins, used for ferrying people up and down the river on holidays.

I knew the Lord was saying "Your circumstances are known to Me, I'm showing you this. Remember the mist in the vision? That was all the cloud you flew through crossing into the USSR."

A knock on the door. Who can it be? We both expected to see a KGB Policeman there asking us to come in for further questioning. However, it was a member of the group saying that the bus was ready for our tour of the city.

Neither of us remembers much about Khabarovsk, being quite devastated with shock and apprehension. I remember that the guide said, regarding the winter, "If you are coming to visit us, it is good to come in December, it is only minus 20C, but don't come in January or February, because it gets to minus 40C, and has been as low as minus 56C.

As far as Doug and I were concerned, we didn't want to come and visit anyway, all we wanted to do was get out of the place. When we arrived back at the Hotel, our room seemed the same. We had lunch, and thank God the bus arrived to take us to the Siberian Railway. What a relief when the train pulled out of the station. Praise God, we weren't going to prison after all, at least not yet!

# The Trans Siberian Railway

SIBERIA .... USSR .... EXILE .... SALT MINES
.... PUNISHMENT .... LONELY GRAVES ....
MYSTERIOUS TRACKLESS WASTES .... DES-
OLATION .... FIERCE MONGOLIAN TRIBES-
MEN GALLOPING ON HORSEBACK .... THE
TRANS SIBERIAN RAILWAY.

That's what Siberia meant to me!

The Railway was built in the late 19th, early 20th
centuries, and stretches from Vladivostok to Moscow.
The gauge is 5' and over 7,000kms is electrified ('80,
I think it is fully electrified now), leaving at that time
1,000kms to go. The train is generally boarded at the
city of Khabarovsk, or from the port of Nahodka, as
Vladivostok is a closed military port. It is the longest
train we have ever travelled on, nineteen carriages,
and we were relieved to feel it move out from the platform after our ordeal at the border.

The trains are comfortable, divided into three
classes, "Soft", "Hard" and "Russian". Tourists are
not permitted to travel in the Russian class. In the
Socialist regime, the classes cannot be named "First"
and "Second", no one is a "second" class citizen in
the USSR.

The "Soft" class cabins contain two berths, the
"Hard" four. There is no sex segretation. A woman
friend of ours found herself sharing a cabin with one
other woman and two men, one of whom was a French
Priest. The Russians are packed in together somewhat
like sardines.

We shared a cabin with another Christian couple,
and found the arrangement pleasant and workable.

We began a prayer chain which continued twenty
four hours a day every moment we travelled. We took
half hour turns and alerted the next one to pray all

through the night and day. This continued from Khabarovsk to the Finnish Border. We claimed the land for the Lord all the way, praying mainly in the Spirit. As someone said, it was like opening up the USSR with a giant zip.

At each stop all day and well into the night, we alighted from the train and as the Scripture says in Joshua 1:3 "Every place the sole of your foot shall touch will be given you." We claimed the USSR for the Lord and His glory.

The Lord also revealed to us that we were "Bearing the Ark across the USSR." This was true, because God's presence traversed the whole of Asia and Europe in us, as we travelled in the train.

Whether or not the carriages are clean depends on the conscientiousness of the attendants. Our two carriage attendants were young men, not at all fussy, and the washrooms, including toilets, were far from clean. The carpet squares in between the berths had absorbed much vodka, grease, food and other dubious matter over the years, and felt so foul underfoot that we folded ours and stacked it under one of the bunks. It also smelt.

There is a strange variety of scanty bed linen, and smooth cotton towels made of fabric like our tea towels. However, they were freshly laundered, and we were sympathetic, as the Russian people are very poor on the whole, and they did their best to make us comfortable.

In each carriage is a coal-fired samovar containing boiling water, from which we made countless cups of "Chai" (tea), and coffee.

Food is loaded aboard the train at the beginning of the trip, and replenished on route. Often we saw the kitchen staff selling food to the peasant people queueing up for hunks of sausage etc. In many ways the

179

train is the life line of these isolated people.

We were allocated a separate restaurant car and three times a day we lurched down the corridors smiling at the Russians and saying "Pshalista" (Please), as we pushed past, "Spaceebo" (Thankyou), as they moved, "Dobray Ootra" (Good morning), or just making friendly sounds and smiles and encouraging noises. I couldn't help thinking that if we'd been dogs we would all be wagging our tails madly and giving short friendly yaps. We loved them, and were really reaching out, and they wanted to be friendly, but how can one form a deep relationship knowing very few words other than "Niet" (no), "Morogane" (pronounced Mahrozhehnahyeh), (Ice Cream), and another word for Watermelon, which I have already forgotten.

Each time we staggered down the swaying train to the dining car they all smiled at us, and we at them. There was a longing to reach out to one another, but an additional inhibiting factor was the number of police on the train, whose job was to keep an eye on us and make sure we didn't indoctrinate any of the locals with our western ways. The Russians bought food on the train which was delivered to them in their compartments in metal containers, so they didn't mix with us in the dining room. Others brought their own food aboard, or bought from the stalls at various stops en route.

The carriages are linked together with rather frightening humped iron plates, and the rocking of the train, the clattering of the wheels and the sight of the ground rushing past made walking rather unpleasant. I'm sure that a blast of icy Siberian winter wind at minus 40C would discourage most people from a constitutional stroll. We were pleased it was summer.

The food was more than adequate, far more than we were used to, or needed, but eating was one of the few activities on the train, so we all overate and most of us put on weight. One girl said to me "I can't fit into my jeans anymore," the price to pay for heavy rye bread and cheese. Buttons strained.

Bread, bread and more bread.

Bread every meal, heavy and generally stale. It sat in heaps on glass dishes, sometimes covered with a cotton cloth, and sometimes left to dry out in the air, but it remained on the dishes until all was eaten. A typical menu was:

Breakfast - Bread, mineral water/fruit juice, herrings, cheese and butter, semolina (with butter, no milk or sugar), fried egg and bacon, tea (chai).

Lunch - Bread, mineral water/syruppy lemonade or beer, cucumber salad, borsch soup, chicken and rice, pastry, biscuits, chai.

Dinner - Bread, mineral water/beer, herring, beef steak and potato, salad (tomato and cucumber, eschalots, sour cream,) biscuits, chai.

There was no choice between tea and coffee. On the rare nights when coffee was served, it was virtually impossible to get a cup of tea. Coffee was on the menu, and that was it!

The train stops at dozens of small stations all along the route, for anything from two to twenty minutes and passengers may climb down and walk about, speak to other passengers or the locals who come down to meet the train. The train is the only contact many of the peasants would have with the outside world in winter, it is their very life blood, carrying food, medicines, etc. There are no major roads into Siberia. The train is the only means of crossing the country.

Many peasant women in cotton dresses, cardigans and head scarves (in summer), sell local produce in small stalls. Russians queue for strange and doubtful-looking cuts of cold fatty meat, buns, biscuits and greasy doughnuts, as well as tomatoes, cucumbers, hot potatoes and bottles of warm flat lemonade. We mainly bought ice cream, when obtainable, just pointed at what we wanted and held out money - universal language!

The train starts without warning bell or whistle, so it is not wise to venture far.

The temperature in Khabarovsk, 500,000 population ('80), ranges from as high as 38° in summer to minus 38° in winter (average). There is practically no stock to be seen in Far Eastern Siberia because of the severe winter conditions. The peasants are poor, the houses very small, and there are no barns for housing animals. The wood for fuel is stacked close to the house, and forms a type of fence, and probably wind-break, until burnt, head-high to reach out of the snow.

There is very little agriculture of any sort in this part of the country. The main industry seems to be timber cutting, and the goods trains pass regularly every 13-15 minutes stacked with logs, 50 to 80 carriages in length.

Hilly forests of beautiful silver birch trees extend for miles and miles from Khabarovsk, their silver and black trunks gleaming in the moonlight. Larch trees also abound. These gradually thin into grassy valleys where farmlets and collectives cluster in friendly groups. Road networks are virtually non-existant in this area. Riddled with potholes, the dirt tracks are quagmires in spring and autumn, dust bowls in summer and snow covered in winter.

We reached the shores of Lake Baikal about 4am, still dark, the largest fresh water lake in the world. It is fed by 300 rivers, and emptied by only 1, on which there are hydro-electric plants. Doug rose at 4am and watched the rounding of the lake in the early dawn.

Irkoutsk is the capital of Eastern Siberia, and is situated near the shore of the lake, and it was here we alighted for a rest after three days and nights aboard the train. It is a city of 750,000, the traditional place of exile in the USSR.

The little wooden houses are like log cabins with double windows and doors because of the intense cold. They also have shutters which are painted either blue or green (the Orthodox Church colours), with white window sills.

In Irkoutsk we were informed by the manager of the Hotel and the Police that they were aware we were a Christian group, and were carrying Bibles. Some had been found and handed in at stations along the route, and if we didn't comply with their demands and hand over all our Bibles we would be escorted to the border as soon as we arrived in Moscow. We sadly handed over all our precious scriptures and prayed that the Lord would keep them safe and not allow them to be burnt. We were allowed to keep one English Bible each.

One small Bible, in pieces and held together with an elastic band, was handed back. The Russian said "That's not worth anything." This raised our hopes that they would be sold on the black market, as they are valuable in the USSR. It costs a man six weeks wages to buy a Bible, if he is able to find one for sale.

As we prayed I saw walls of fire, not to burn the Bibles, but to protect them.

After leaving Irkoutsk we showed our true colours. We had been hiding our faith as much as possible until this point, but now that the Bibles had been taken we had nothing to lose. For the next three days and nights we gathered once or twice a day in the corridor of our carriage, and sang choruses and praised the Lord. A few Russians stood and listened. We now approached Russians on the platform and said

"Christos voscress" (Christ is risen), and "Eesoos vas lubeet", (Jesus loves you), "Bog vas lubeet" (God loves you "Ya vas lubeet" (I love you), and gave them bookmarks and cards with Christian messages and pictures on them. The people themselves are very open and need love so badly.

The younger members of the group had produced frizbees at the stations, catching and throwing to one another and to any others who would like to participate. The Russians loved it, and some did join in while others stood around in groups watching. They are a very sad oppressed people, smile rarely, although they are warm and passionate. They were impressed with the joy of the Christians, and said so. Some of our lads also played chess in the dining room with Russians and others took their guitars into the Russian's cabins and sang songs.

When Sunday came we were given permission to have a Christian service in the dining car, and actually took Communion crossing the Volga. The dining room staff gathered at the far end of the carriage and watched and listened. When we were coming into a station they pulled down the blinds .....(for fear, or to save contaminating the Russians?)

As the train stood at each major station, railway hands tapped each wheel hub. It seemed strange to see Russian women in greasy overalls and head scarves doing these dirty menial jobs, but of course this is all part of their "equality".

The women also "watered" the train at various points, attaching big hoses to pipes under the platform and turning water cocks to fill the kitchen and washroom tanks under the carriages. Women also used sledgehammers and changed points. They oiled the tracks, carrying large greasy cans. I must say I found the use of women in this way quite appalling, yet wondered if it is really as bad as the way women are exploited as sex objects in Amsterdam, or Australia for that matter.

Two women attendants travelled with us from Irkoutsk to Moscow. Our party boarded carrying dettol, clean rags, soap etc. and immediately cleaned the carriage tables, toilet and washroom and even the windows. Everything smelt of dettol and looked sparkling clean. The attendants were amazed but quite concerned when we rolled up the mats and hid them out of sight.

In one of the carriages the previous passenger had been storing a large fish under the berth for some days in the summer heat. It had left a pool of liquid and a very strong fishy smell which didn't improve the odour of the floor mat. The couple in this cabin asked the attendants to store the carpet down in their quarters, which they agreed to do after the couple threatened the throw it out the window.

A very drunk Russian male boarded the train at one station, and I wondered how our woman attendant would deal with the situation. He was a big man, and I felt sure she'd call for assistance. Not a bit of it! She wheeled that man around and had him off the train so quickly!

When the train stopped at red signal lights, and flowers were seen, ·the more venturesome males aboard jumped down and gathered handfuls of beautiful wildflowers, with one eye on the signals, accompanied by loud cheers and encouragements from passengers leaning out of windows. When the lights changed to green there was a mad scramble to jump aboard, as the train moves off silently. The bottom step is a few feet from the ground and difficult to scale, but we didn't lose anybody and our compartments were bright with flowers.

The hills became more gentle, and the forest less dense as we crossed large rivers and the Russian steppes to Novosibirsk, the Capital of Western Siberia. Over 1,000,000 people live in this city on the banks of the Ob River. Temperatures of minus 45°C have been recorded here, but the citizens are proud of their ability to withstand such conditions.

Everywhere men and women and often whole families were scything, working from dawn to dark gathering hay for the long winter. The hay was stored in big ricks with a long pointed stick in the centre about four metres high, so that the hay stack could be found under snow. Animals were more prevalent in this part of the country.

As we approached the Ural Mountains, which are really undulating hills just here, we noticed avalanche shelters built across the tracks in several places where we ran close to the hillside.

These are big concrete re-inforced platforms over the tracks where rocks and snow might slide down.

After crossing the Urals the hills gave way to flat country, and eventually to the marshy terrain surrounding Moscow. For nearly an hour coming into Moscow there is not one house. Everyone lives in units in Moscow, most of them grey. There is very little colour.

We were sad to leave the rocking of the train and the life on board, the magnificent forests and terrain of Siberia, but Moscow held a new challenge and we stepped thoughtfully, if not eagerly, onto the Moscow platform, into the very heart of the Soviet Union.

# i) Moscow

Apart from Red Square, Moscow is grey. Her buildings are drab, her people sad, and her spirit is joyless and depressed. There is a prevailing air of hopelessness. Moscow is grey.

The people have a dull indoctrinated pride. "This is Lenin's Tomb", they boast. "This is the Kremlin." "Mr Breshnev ('80) comes to work in this building nearly every day." "This is the Museum of ......", "In this building is the Academy of Science." "Here is another statue of Lenin." But their hearts are heavy, their eyes are lifeless, they are deprived and oppressed and fearful.

They say flatly "There is no God", but God is love, and here in Moscow there is no love, no joy, no peace as we Christians know it. "Look at beautiful Red Square," they say, and it certainly is splendid to behold, but the spirit of oppression and death hangs heavily over the cobbled grey square.

Red Square is bounded on one end by a large red brick building, a Science Museum bent on proving that man is supreme, without God.

Along one adjoining side runs a high red wall, beyond which is the Kremlin. Lenin's Tomb in red and black marble stands in the Square. Every hour the guard is changed on the tomb to protect the dead body of Lenin. The guard marches out the Kremlin gate, along Red Square to the Tomb with the sickening rhythmical thud of the goose step, a fearful sound. Everywhere is a show of strength striking fear deep into the heart.

Overlooking the Square from the Kremlin hangs the Red Flag of the USSR, and a large red star weighing nearly three quarters of a ton, lit from within at night, is poised on top of one of the Kremlin Towers. This is the five-pointed star of Communism.

On the other end of Red Square is the spectacular, but pagan-influenced Cathedral of St. Basil. The

Communist Government has long since turned it into a tourist attraction. It has an eastern barbaric splendour about it, but was never significant as a House of God. It was built by Tsar Ivan the Terrible to commemorate his victory over the Tartars, and so pleased was he with its beauty that he had the architect's eyes put out so that he would never again design a building so splendid. The interior is heavily decorated, oriental, pagan looking, containing eight chapels.

The other side of Red Square is bounded by a huge, magnificent building, ornate and beautiful, which houses Moscow's largest department store, and a large Intourist hotel.

Shopping in Moscow is strange. The department store mentioned above is structured in three long arcades. They are three stories high with barrelled roofs of glass, running the full length of the building.

There are no advertisements and very few signs. The store is divided into many small stores each containing its own specialised wares - glasses in one, china in another, shoes in another etc.; but as the Government owns them all there is no competition, no need to advertise. There is very little choice. When a popular item is on sale, the queues are unbelievably long. We saw queues of about 30 or 40 women lined up for plain yellow "T" shirts. In many shops the shelves are nearly bare.

Near the shops, on the corner of Red Square, are about ten dispensers where one puts in two kopeks (about four cents Aust.), presses a button, and cold mineral water fills a glass. It is delicious. The glass is left on the machine, and when pressed face down on the faucet is washed with jets of water.

On arrival in Moscow we were billeted in an Intourist Hotel, Sevastopol. The tourist hotels have a full-time, twenty-four hour, female attendant on each floor, who actually lives in quarters near her desk. Security measures are very tight, passes must be shown day or night entering or leaving the Hotel. Tickets must be presented for meals.

It was quite an adventure travelling in the lifts, which are often unreliable. One Russian attendant was annoyed because some of us didn't want to use one particular lift that kept breaking down. She said "Why are you so fussy? It works most of the time."

We were informed by our Intourist Guide that there are only about 30,000 cars in Moscow ('80), where the population is 8,500,000. The number of cars is increasing, but most of the people can't afford them, and there are very few new cars. The Government is not wanting people to own cars for economic reasons and say they are trying to keep the pollution levels down, no doubt also trying to save fuel by encouraging the people to use the excellent railway system.

The Moscow Underground Railway system is superb, Lenin having brought the concept from London. It is highly efficient. For five kopeks, or about ten cents Australian, one may travel anywhere in the city or suburbs. The trains leave every few minutes, and are fast moving, comfortable and clean. A recorded voice in Russian and then English gives the name of the Station, then "Mind the doors, next stop......"

The Underground Stations themselves are incredible. Beautiful statues abound. Walls, ceilings, floors are all marble, with chandelier lights and monuments to events or people which are still held in favour by the present political regime. When a person (Stalin for example) falls from grace, all evidence of their previous power is hastily removed.

The escalators are longer and faster than in any

other country I have visited. Stepping on to a downward moving escalator in Moscow is not for the faint hearted.

Another anxiety provoking experience in the Underground is to identify the right line and station. All names are written in Russian, in the Cyriac Alphabet, so one might just as well be attempting to read Chinese or Greek. The Russian Alphabet has more letters than ours, and most of those letters we have in common have different sound. Our "R" is their "P", our "U" is their "Y", our "S" is their "C" etc. My name "Ruth" is spelt "Pyt" in Russian.

One generally has the names of the stations printed carefully in strange "hieroglyphics" on a piece of paper, often clutched in feverish hand, holding it up against the notice board with puzzled look. A foreigner stands out like a sore thumb in Moscow, but the people are kind, and often an English-speaking Russian will come over and say "May I help you?"

The Intourist guides and attendants really did their best to make our stay in Moscow enjoyable, and cause us to feel welcome. They are friendly and loving people and we warmed to them, and longed to witness to them of our loving God and Saviour. Witnessing became a way of life.

We tried to lose no opportunity to witness. It was strange speaking to people in the lifts etc., smiling and saying "Do you speak English?" Sometimes the reply was "Niet", or "Non", or "Nien", sometimes "Yes, I'm British" in Oxford accent.

If the person spoke English we would say "We are a group of Christians travelling around the world telling people Jesus loves them," but if Russian, "Christos voscress" "Christ is risen", and a few other phrases. We witnessed in parks, trains, lifts, restaurants, railway stations, and we grew to love it.

"Witnessing is a way of life" became our motto, our "Magnificent Obsession."

The parks and gardens are beautiful, and summer is the best time to see them. In city parks we noticed that when we sat next to a Russian or a group of young people, we were generally being watched. Sometimes a man with a newspaper or book, like an ill-disguised spy, would sit beside us, pretending to read, but obviously listening to our conversation. A pair of new shoes on an otherwise shabbily dressed man is a give-away. I'm sure we were followed a lot more than we realised.

On one suburban train I sat between two women, and a policeman sat next to the woman on my left. As we travelled along I said to the lady on my right "Do you speak English?" She heard me, but gave no indi-cation of it, kept looking straight ahead. I realised she was afraid of the policeman, but he couldn't hear what I was saying, so I said "Christos voscress." No acknowledgement whatsoever. "Eesoos vas lubeet". No flickering of an eyelid, but as I rose to alight she glanced straight into my eyes and smiled quickly.

The day after we arrived in Moscow our group of twenty divided into twos and for two hours walked slowly around the Red Square praying in the Spirit, binding the powers of darkness, and releasing the Lord to move in the people, and in the land. Much prayer was offered up outside Lenin's Tomb, the stronghold of Death in Moscow.

Lenin is revered almost as God. There is a life-sized statue to his glory in almost every public park, and although there are no commercial advertisements in the country, the sayings of Lenin are painted up on display. Everyone is expected to visit Lenin's tomb at least once a year, and view his body. Some of our number lined up at 7.30am till 9am to see his remains, but Doug and I were appalled at the thought. Lining up all that time seemed to us almost like a form of homage, which we weren't prepared to pay.

We saw a man being arrested in Red Square. He was "bundled off" by three burly KGB men, and later the story was told us by a Scottish man who witnessed the whole incident. The British Press Photographers and Journalists were waiting to interview Wells, the British runner who later won a Gold Medal. Suddenly the man, an Italian, began to demonstrate by shouting loudly against the system. His two friends were homosexuals, and had been arrested by the Russians and gaoled for three months. Immediately he began to shout the KGB descended upon him, and pinning his right hand to his left shoulder they raced him across the Square so quickly his feet nearly left the ground. He was pale with fear. The British Press took photos, but KGB men grabbed their cameras and tore out the films.

The man was pushed into a car with darkened windows, which immediately sped out of the Square. We could have taken pictures of the arrest, but weighed the possibility of losing all that was on our film, and decided against it.

Space will not permit me to describe in detail the sights and events we saw in Moscow.

The Kremlin was the original walled city of Moscow, built about 1200. The city was bounded by the Moscow River and another smaller stream which is crossed by a bridge, and guarded by a Watchtower. The stream has since been covered over and become a path.

In the Kremlin is the Tsar's Summer Palace, a magnificent building, and five Cathedrals, two of which were for the Tsar's personal use, one for private worshipping with his family, the other for

Coronations, not quite so personal. All five Cathedrals are now Museums or just Tourist attractions.
The Russian Cabinet works in the Offices of State
within the Kremlin. The buildings spread outwards
from the walled city to become Moscow as we know it
today.

The Kremlin Theatre is now the Opera House of
Russia, and lies within the walls. It is a superb building holding 5,500 people in the largest Auditorium.
Doug and I saw the Bolshoi Ballet perform here, and
we were enraptured not only with the Ballet, but also
with the building. At the interval many people surge
aboard the wonderful express escalators and four of
these take one up to the Supper Room. Here theatre
goers mix with ease queueing at the various signs
"Chai" (tea), "Morogane" (ice cream) etc.

I witnessed to a beautiful Russian woman in the Ice
Cream queue, "Christos voscress". Tears came to her
eyes as she took my hand, squeezed it warmly and
smiled. We couldn't converse, but real love passed between us.

On another occasion I visited the Moscow Circus,
which I found most enjoyable, but the most interesting
event of our visit to Moscow was attending the
Olympic Games.

Our motivation for coming to the USSR was to
show love and joy to the Russian people, and the
Games made it possible for us to be so open about our
Christian witness. Russia opened her arms to other
nations at this time, and even built a Chapel to seat 500
at Olympic Village, for all religions. Christians from
all over the world came to witness their faith.

We were grieved to see many rebellious people
from countries whose leaders had asked them not to
attend, and were embarrassed to feel many would put
us in this category, but we were called by a Higher

Authority than an earthly leader, many months before Afghanistan events happened, and He verified the call to the end.

Our tickets for the track events had been allocated weeks before, including the seat positions, but I knew by the Vision I originally received that the bowl containing the Olympic Flame would be up high on our left. It was.

The boycott of the Games was witnessed by those who attended. Great blocks of empty seats, never shown on Television, bore silent testimony to the strong protest of USA, Great Britain, West Germany, Japan, France, Holland etc, to the invasion of Afghanistan.

The absence of the great athletes from the USA and other world powers reduced the competitive standard of the Games, which of course are meant to be world wide. Many events were totally won by the Communist Block, but there were so few countries participating that this was almost a farce.

It was disappointing to see that bunting replaced the National flags, which would have been flown from the staffs around the main stadium. When an athlete stands on the dais to receive a medal, his national flag is raised and the national anthem played.

However, for example, when Wells from Great Britain stood to receive his gold medal, the Olympic flag went up and some inconsequential music played. We were longing to see the Union Jack raised, and hear the British National Anthem, but Britain was not an officially participating nation. We noticed him wipe away a tear - was it joy, or was he grieved that he couldn't represent his country in this his hour of doubtful triumph?

When Wells ran the race which won him the Gold Medal, he wanted to continue a "Victor's circuit" of the track, receiving the acclaim of the crowd, but the Russian officials tried to stop him. He dodged two men and kept running, but they formed a line right across the track and prevented him from going further. Order must be kept in crowds at all times.

We visited three practicing Orthodox Churches. They were heavily embossed inside with gold, and many icons hung on the walls, some very old and priceless. In one church there were middle-aged women wearing black head scarves, sweeping the floor with hand-made brush brooms, and one other woman dusting the furniture. We managed to leave two Gospels of John on one of the shelves, and prayed that the right people would find them.

We didn't attend a service as they are Russian spoken and everyone stands for one hour. I find standing for that length of time tiring. (There are no chairs!) The two Baptist Churches in Moscow cater for 8,500,000 people. We attempted to attend a service, but were given a bogus address. Some of our members attended a young people's sing-along, which they enjoyed. These are the registered churches.

I find it difficult to understand the difference between the "Unregistered" Churches and the "Underground" Church. Both hold meetings in secret, generally in private homes or forests. The leaders are all "wanted" because holding unregistered services is "against the system". There are no registered Sunday Schools or Youth Meetings or Outreaches. The young Russians must not be indoctrinated by false beliefs, and it is a crime to teach children things spiritual. "There is no God."

We were sad when it came time to leave Moscow, for we felt that we had achieved so little when it came to witnessing, because of the language barrier, but the Holy Spirit can use our little loaves and fishes, and multiply them. We believe for it. The main reason for our visit to the USSR had nevertheless been achieved. The people and their land were indelibly written on our hearts for prayer and intercession. Russia, we will never forget you, we love you.

## j) To Leningrad and the Border

What a strange thing. We travelled all the way to Leningrad backwards! On our train, all seats faced Moscow.

On this train we were able to mix freely with the Russians, which was good, and Doug and I decided to separate in the dining car. I sat opposite two young men, Pietra (Peter) and Vladimir. They couldn't speak a word of English, and I had only about ten Russian words, but somehow we had an animated conversation saying practically nothing, but laughing a lot. Everything we said was interspersed with "Niet panny mieu," "I don't understand," and more laughs.

I heard a commotion at the table across the aisle and looked over just in time to see an inebriated Russian ex-serviceman (wearing his medals), grab Doug and embrace him heartily, kissing him soundly on both cheeks. Before Doug had time to recover from this, he poured a glass of vodka or similar beverage, with unsteady hand, and perhaps aided by a jerk of the train, lurched forward and tipped the contents of the glass into Doug's lap.

Apparently we made quite an impression, because another Russian passenger, Tanya, asked if we would sign the Visitor's Book, which she assured us they kept for Important People. We both signed and wrote "Christos voscress" and "Praise the Lord."

When tea was served, it was brought with a whole round slice of preserved orange, in syrup. Delicious!

Another strange experience happened when witnessing to a University student. He had been studying English, and really spoke quite fluently. We conversed about his course, and when it was time to leave I thought I'd say a few words about Jesus, so looked him straight in the eyes and said "Christos voscress, Eesoos vas lubeet." Later the penny dropped, and I thought '"Why on earth did I witness to him in Russian when we had been speaking in English together for about ten minutes." Maybe the Holy Spirit caught his attention this way.

And so we arrived at beautiful Leningrad, formerly St. Petersburg, ancient city of Peter the Great, and former capital of Russia. Here one may see the Winter Palace of the Tsars, the Political Prison on an island near the Cathedral of St. Peter and St. Paul, lovely bridges over Leningrad's many scenic waterways, and grand buildings, many of which bear bullet and shell holes as a grim reminder of war.

City of sorrow. City of the Great Seige, when over one million citizens were killed or starved or froze to death in one horrific winter at the beginning of the Second World War. The seige by the Nazis lasted 900 gruelling days, '41-'43. In 1907 the people's liberation struggle culminated in the great October Socialist Revolution. The victory was won by the Communist Party under the leadership of Vladimir Illyick Lenin, and the world's first socialist state was founded, the Union of Soviet Socialist Republics.

St. Petersburg was renamed Leningrad in Lenin's honour. After Finland threw off the Russian yoke, the city was seen to be too vulnerable, being so close to the border, and so Moscow became the new capital.

Surely one of the most beautiful hotels in Russia is the Pribaltiyskaya, meaning "By the side of the Baltic." We stayed here for two nights. It was designed by Finnish architects and built by Swedish builders, and is superb. The Hotel is a showpiece not only for tourists, but also an example of the high standard of Western building.

Because the Russians may not travel to the Capitalist countries, except under special conditions, the builders never see how our buildings are finished. Standards are very shoddy, quite unacceptable in our own country. In one hotel we pulled out the basin plug and the water came up through the floor, and the toilet consistently leaked at the base. Many doors would not shut and the paint had dribbled before it dried, for just a few examples.

However, builders and architects and decorators from all over the country may visit the Pribaltiyskaya, and be inspired to higher standards. There is also a new high quality hotel just opened in Moscow and one or two others in the Black Sea holiday area, but they have only recently been built ('80).

The sky was still light at 10.30pm, being midsummer. Doug was busy, so I walked alone down to the shore of the Bay of Finland, which is what this part of the Baltic is named, to take a photo of the last pink rays from the setting sun. Many people were out walking in the warm night air. Gradually I became aware that I was being followed. I increased my pace. So did he. I wasn't afraid because there were lots of people around, so I stopped and admired the view till he either caught up or passed.

He was grey haired, with a poised military bearing, and he clicked his heels and bowed from the waist, addressing me in Russian. I said "Niet panny mieu," "I don't understand, do you speak English? Angliski? Parlez vous Francaise?" He spoke Russian, German, Bulgarian, Czechoslovakian and Polish, but not English or French. This was quite a culture shock for me. I thought that anyone who was at all educated spoke either English or French.

He then produced his Hotel Identity Card, and pointed to his name. I couldn't read it. He also pointed to his room number. I said "Niet, niet", somewhat hastily, and showed him my wedding ring. I tried to think of some recognisable word in Latin or German or French for "husband". Impossible. Pointing towards the Hotel I said "My husband is here and is coming soon," but of course he didn't understand, or pretended he didn't.

Language barriers can be so frustrating. He pointed once more to the room number. "Niet, niet." Conversation was impossible, but I was able to convey those wonderful words "Christos voscress, Eesoos vas lubeet." He looked at me impassively, clicked his heels, bowed once again as he kissed my hand, and walked off into the night. I believe though, that the Holy Spirit will give him light. I prayed, believing, for his salvation.

Jesus loves a Ruski (Russian), even if he belongs to the KGB, which I suspect he did.

The following day we boarded the train for Helsinki. We sang Christian songs on the Leningrad platform accompanied by guitar. Many Russians stood watching and listening. We were all close to tears, including Natasha, our apparently unshakeable Communist guide, to whom we were singing farewell. She hastily wiped her eyes.

Once more we were separated from the rest of the train, with one other passenger - a Finnish girl. When we arrived at the border the train was stopped, and Customs Police entered our carriage. All windows and doors were locked, including the toilets, for nearly an hour. The sun beat down on the carriage roof, and the midsummer heat was stifling.

Customs men went through all our possessions with a fine tooth comb. It is difficult to know what they were looking for, perhaps names and addresses of Christians or Underground Church meeting places. We carried no information.

We also had to account for every dollar taken into the country, and every one spent. Police are watching for people dealing on the black market. Russians pay a lot of money for used jeans. They come up to tourists wearing jeans and ask to buy what they are wearing. Customs men are also probably looking for drugs.

When the last case was searched, and the last passenger interrogated, they unlocked the doors and windows, and left the carriage. The train began to move, and crossed the border slowly. We threw open the windows, and as we crossed it was like coming out of a prison into sunshine. A great oppressive weight lifted from our spirits. We sang and danced and hugged one another and laughed. What a wonderful release.

I will never forget the joy we felt arriving at the next station, in Finland. The seats were painted bright blue, brilliant flowers in brightly coloured pots decorated the platform. The restaurant too was decked in colour, such a change from the drab greys of the USSR. There were colourful advertisements and curtains and delicious cakes for sale and sweets in coloured wrappings. It was all such a contrast, and what we normally take for granted in our western culture was fresh and exciting.

We went into the washroom and found they had warm water and real toilet paper and soap too, and plugs in the wash basins.

It is difficult to describe the joy of being free, after the oppression we had been subject to. Oh the wonders of living in a country where one has freedom of choice. Praise God. Let us appreciate what He has given us and love Him for it. Free will is one of God's greatest blessings to man. Our free will may be bound by other men, or by evil spirits. When we walk with the Lord He gives us freedom.

"Where the Spirit of the Lord is, there is freedom." 2 Cor 3:17 NIV.

# k) The Persecuted Church

The cry of the persecuted Church reaches up to heaven:

"Why have You rejected us, O God,
Why does Your anger smoulder?
Remember us Lord, Your people.

Look at all this destruction in the land.
Your foes roared in the sanctuary where we worshipped You,
They smashed the beautiful interiors,
They burned Your churches,
They said in their hearts 'We will crush them completely.'

Why Lord, why?

We are given no miraculous signs,
No prophets are left, and we don't know how long this will be.

How long Lord? Why do You withhold Your hand, Lord?

But Lord, all power is Yours,
Remember how Your Name is mocked and reviled.
Do not handed over the life of your dove to wild beasts.

Do not forget the lives of Your afflicted people for
   ever.
Remember Your covenant, because haunts of
   violence fill the dark places of the land.
Do not let the oppressed retreat in disgrace, may
   we praise Your Name.
Rise up, O God, and defent Your cause."

(Parts of Psalm 74 NIV paraphrased)

## l) What can we do to help the Russian Church?

On returning home, we feel almost a part of the
persecuted Church. We long to speak once more to the
people, and tell them Jesus loves them. Our hearts
reach out to them in the only possible way - prayer.

Often I thank the Lord that we are waking up in a
warm comfortable bed. I thank God that I am here at
home, with Doug beside me, not over there in a cold
prison, suffering God only knows what!

The temperature in Siberia as I write in early
winter, is approaching minus 20°C, and the prisons
are not likely to be centrally heated. The blankets
would be few, the food inadequate.

"Lord please bless and care for our brothers and
sisters in prison, their only 'crime' being that they
love You. Help us to remember to pray for them
Lord."

I once heard the testimony of an airman who spent
the night in freezing cold on the side of a mountain in
Turkey. As it snowed he felt he would die of cold, but
in answer to his prayer, the Lord sent an angel, which
wrapped its wings around him and kept him warm all
night. I just pray that the Lord will send angels to
those in prison in the USSR who are suffering from

the cold, and that they may know that it is the Lord Jesus Who sent them.

I praise the Lord for the understanding He has given us of the persecuted Church, and the communion of saints, all over the world.

It was good to arrive home via Great Britain, Amsterdam, over the Pole to Los Angeles, thence to Auckland and Sydney.

We shared Russian experiences with Roger and Margie, who had been witnessing in the Black Sea area of the USSR, with the Australian YWAM team, and all agreed that Jesus, the Holy Spirit, and freedom of choice are the Father's greatest gift to men.

# Chapter 22
# Healing (Bowel)

Back home in Sydney I had another remarkable healing. At twenty, during the '39-'45 war, I was serving in the WAAAF, and one morning was struck by an acute pain in my right side. Appendicitis, I thought, and raced off to Sick Parade.

I was at this time on the current "Crash Diet" for losing weight, Epsom salts and lemon taken first thing in the morning on an empty stomach. This had quite a violent effect on the bowel, to say the least, but as my mother always said "Beauty feels no pain," and as long as I was losing weight nothing else mattered.

On this particular morning I found it difficult to walk, the right leg being affected. The doctors were mystified, and on hearing my cough, said I'd probably torn a muscle in my stomach coughing. In other words they didn't know what the trouble was, and I decided to ignore it and hope it would go away.

The discomfort was intermittent, but tended to increase as I grew older, until in 1980-81, I was having periods of up to 5 or 6 days when there was a total bowel blockage. Even gas couldn't get through, it would reach the area in the lower bowel, and then bubble back along the bowel sounding, as my husband said, "like a blocked sink". At this stage I was afraid of cancer, but after all my other healings was prepared to trust God. The pain was a real "stopper". When a wave of pain hit me I couldn't even move until it passed, it was so severe.

During one of these painful blockages I was praying for healing, and reading John 5:6 "When Jesus saw him lying there, and knew that he had been in that condition a long time, He said to him 'Do you want to be made well?'" These words suddenly seemed alive to me, Jesus was speaking to me right at that moment, and I said "Yes Lord, I do, I desperately do!"

Then the verse above claimed my attention v5: "Now a certain man was there who had an infirmity thirty eight years", and the Holy Spirit reminded me "You were twenty when you first noticed the problem, and now you're fifty eight, like the man in the story you've been in that condition thirty eight years."

Praise God, my faith level soared, and I was healed, have only had an occasional slight pain, no real blockages, since that time five years ago. The Holy Spirit also at that time showed me to eat bran, which has helped greatly.

# Chapter 23
# Mummy's Death

My mother was a sprightly young eighty five, still driving her own car, so occupied with her social life I had to almost make an appointment to visit her.

The last time I saw her conscious was a Saturday afternoon, when she drove down to visit Doug and me for afternoon tea. To my surpise she handed me a paper headed "At my death", a distribution of jewellery, with a list of beneficiaries.

I was surprised as she never spoke of dying, the subject was taboo, and so I said "Mummy, fancy you talking about dying," and she replied "I'm getting very old you know."

This was the Holy Spirit preparing her no doubt. The following Saturday, she informed us she had a card party, and couldn't keep our usual appointment for afternoon tea. Unfortunately she apparently had a stroke coming on gradually, and lost her way in the car for the first time driving over to Northbridge, although she had travelled this route many times before. She played a good game of bridge, drove home, parked the car in the garage, turned on the stove to make a cup of tea, but forgot to light the gas, and went to bed.

In the morning neighbours smelt gas, found her unconscious, called the Ambulance, which raced her to hospital, where we visited her.

When I was a little girl we lived by the sea, and on a moonlit night I often would say "Mummy, come and see the moonlight on the water," and she would say "Isn't it beautiful?" As I prayed for her now, Jesus gave me a vision. I saw the lovely moonlight on the water scene as I had seen it as a child, but slowly, very slowly, a large ship was moving into the moonlight. I knew in my spirit that it represented my mother, that as the ship would very slowly pass through the moonlight and out into the darkness, so would my mother slowly pass away.

Doug and I had an appointment at a healing service at Penshurst that afternoon, and as we took our seats I noticed a picture on the wall. It was a moonlight scene of the sea, just the same as in my vision, but the figure of Jesus was in it. He was saying "Don't be afraid, I'm in this." I remembered Jesus speaking to me eighteen months previously about my mother. I was praying for her salvation (which she confidently resisted, saying she'd lived a good life, and didn't need it), and He showed me words on a little sticker "Expect a miracle".

Each day I visited my mother and spoke directly into her ear. She was in a coma, but the Sister attending her said "She can hear you. I tell her when I'm about to move her, wash her etc., because I know she can hear me."

I spoke into my mother's ear "Mummy, you need Jesus, He is the One Who will take you to Heaven. He will forgive your sins, confess them to Him, ask for forgiveness. He said 'I am the Door; by Me.....you will enter in and be saved'. John 10:9. Mummy, you need Jesus."

I also prayed in tongues directly into her ear. A person in a coma may have lost the use of their brain, but the spirit still lives within and knows what is going on. When the spirit leaves, the person dies. That is death, the final separation of the spirit from the body.

On the third day, reading Mark on my way to work on the bus, I came to Mark 9:1 "There are some standing here who will not taste death till they see the Kingdom of God present with power." The Holy Spirit said, "she will not die till she sees Jesus and speaks with Him."

Praise God, she passed away some hours later, straight into the presence of the Saviour she'd only just met. This should be an encouragement to all who visit the unconscious. Speak into their ear, who knows, they may have a union with Jesus before they die.

At the funeral I meant to ask for the hymn "Jesus, the very thought of Thee," but by the Spirit chose "How sweet the Name of Jesus sounds in a believer's ear." One of my daughters said to me later "You must have chosen that specially, Mum, 'In a believer's ear'!"

Later I realised the succeeding verses to Mark 9:1 are the description of the Transfiguration of Jesus on the Mount, and I believe that that was how mummy saw Him, in His shining, transfigured form. Praise God. You said "Expect a Miracle," and You gave it!

# Chapter 24
# Music

I write this not to in any way exhalt myself, but to encourage any who may have musical talent which the Lord is longing to use.

I began piano lessons at about six years of age, but as I grew older and more sensitive became acutely uncomfortable performing in public, with such anxiety and fear that my hands would shake almost uncontrollably.

I won the Senior Scholarship for Music at school, and played often for assembly and Sunday services etc., but this award entailed playing two pieces on Speech Day for the assembled school, parents and friends, the School Board (one of whom had donated the Scholarship), plus teaching staff, some two thousand people. So afraid was I of this performance, I went to the Headmistress and pleaded to be allowed to forego the Scholarship, in order to dodge the dreaded Speech Day performance. She refused.

Thank God I played well on the dreaded day, but left the hall in tears, shaking violently with nerves. I passed my Leaving Certificate with first class honours in Music, and then dropped music out of my life.

All this time I could only play without music if I'd learned the piece "by rote" as it were, with much practice, and couldn't play a note without the musical score. For over thirty years I hardly opened the lid of the piano, but by now a Christian, when I heard the parable of the talents my spirit stirred within me, and the Holy Spirit challenged me.

"Lord, You know I can't play without music, and

even then my sight-reading is so poor. I need to stumble around and practice for hours before I can play."

"Ruth, I've given you a musical talent."

During this time I'd played hymns often at Church on the harmonium, and even bought a reed organ with two registers, an automatic pump, full pedal board, and had eighteen months organ tuition, but always playing from music.

Then I was baptised in the Holy Spirit. (He makes all the difference in every area of our life.)

"Lord, I would love You to release my piano playing, and I'd play for You Lord, You alone, but I need the gift of playing in the Spirit, without music."

And the Holy Spirit gave me this gift. It happened this way:

I attended one session of a music seminar at the Hordern Pavilion. The speaker asked for anyone present who didn't as yet have a music ministry, but wanted one, to stand. I stood, and was prayed for with all the others standing.

The speaker suggested a very simple chorus, to begin playing without music, one which only contained about three chords:

"Give thanks unto the Lord,
Give thanks unto the Lord,
For His steadfast love endures for ever."

As I sat at the piano I began to realise that the simple chords could be played as appeggios for variation, and that I could acutally accompany the right hand melody with something harmonious in the left. As I did this gradually the Holy Spirit released me.

There were three other significant occasions relating to my release in music. At about this time I asked two friends to pray that I would be given the gift of music. They prayed and I fell to the floor "slain in the Spirit". On another occasion I was sitting at the piano just looking at the keys when the Spirit fell on me. I rested my head and hands on the keys and wept uncontrollably for a few seconds then the joy of the Spirit flooded in, and I knew that the Spirit was bearing witness with my spirit in intercession for the gift.

On the third occasion I was at a Full Gospel Businessmen's evening and there wasn't a pianist. They only wanted a couple of very simple choruses which I knew well, and the two leaders laid hands on me and prayed for a release into a music ministry. For the first time in my life I was able to play without fear and apprehension of hitting a wrong note, and actually played the choruses in a tremendously simple way, without the score.

To begin a music ministry as well as any other ministry we need not only to begin in a small way, but also we must step out in faith. Often this is painful, and there are very few more likely ways of making a fool of oneself than stepping out 'solo' in music. Sometimes the Lord even throws us in at the deep end. This happened to me!

Doug and I were in Brisbane at a Vision Conference. In Festival Hall, during the afternoon seminar, the Pastor in charge said "We don't appear to have a pianist. Is there anyone here who can play the piano?" I waited uneasily for all the pianists to raise their hands. Not one! "Surely there's someone who can play the piano? Oh well (after a long pause), I suppose we'll have to sing without music."

My heart sank. What a struggle within! By faith I was stepping out in music. To say nothing was tantamount to stating "I am not a musician, I cannot play the piano, the Lord is not helping me, I am afraid to step out with the Holy Spirit, I don't want this release

I've been praying so earnestly about." God help me! I walked up to the Pastor "I can play just a little." "Great" he said, "there's the piano."

Oh yes, there it was, on the platform of the Festival Hall, a big concert grand, and not only was I a babe in all this, but I could only play in the key of 'F'.

The Pastor said kindly "Here's the music", but I'd lost my glasses some months previously, was believing for a healing of my eyes, and I couldn't even see the music! "Lord if You don't help me I'm sunk!"

Thank God, everything he asked me to play I managed, all in 'F'. I played for the meetings every afternoon that week.

I was also the only pianist present at the Anglican Cathedral at the Charismatic service, and was asked to play the piano there as well. Jesus said "Come, walk to Me on the water."

Then another "stepping out in faith" at Meroo Conference Centre, where I played the melody and a brother played the bass, on the one piano. There was also a guitarist and organist on this occasion.

And then the Piece de resistance! Horror of horrors! Someone told the organiser of the FGBMFI Banquet at the Chevron Hotel that the music was great at Meroo, and he asked me to play at the coming Banquet.

"Lord, I'm just a baby in music, there must be someone else who can do it. I know this is testing my faith, but Lord this is just too much!"

I asked the organisers to please, please, get someone else, but the weeks passed, and they said "No one else available, you are it!"

To cut a long story short, I arrived early on the night of the Banquet, and began playing before anyone arrived. I didn't dare stop in case I was too nervous to start again, so played till everyone was seated (still in 'F'), without music.

Jimmy Johnson was the speaker, a wonderful American Christian brother, First Secretary for the Navy, in the habit of attending prayer meetings at the White House. After a great address Jimmy began singing "He is Lord." I had prayed that I could start the music off, in 'F' of course. My God! What key is he singing in? I rose from my table, crossed the floor, sat at the piano to accompany him, and, wonderful Holy Spirit, he was singing in my key!

To all who aspire to play for the Lord, step out in faith in the Holy Spirit, it's the only way. I always feel I'm out on a limb when I play, but the Spirit never allows me to fall, or the limb to break.

Music is not my main ministry, and I've hardly been asked to play since, as I have so little time to practice; but now I feel thankful that I ventured out on the call "Come, walk to Me on the water." I only play for my own praise and worship times just now, and also in intercession. God has given me a few tunes and choruses by the Spirit, most of them personal. There is one "Rain Song" He gave me which I play when praying for rain - sounds a little like a Rain Dance doesn't it, but this was given me by the Holy Spirit.

The possibilities of playing in the Spirit are boundless. Reach for it!

# Chapter 25
# Rain

Rain is a blessing from God.
Psalm 65:9-13 NIV:
"You care for the land and water it:
You enrich it abundantly.
The streams of God are filled with water
to provide the people with grain,
for so You have ordained it.

You drench its furrows and level its ridges:
You soften it with showers and bless its crops.
You crown the year with Your bounty,
and Your carts overflow with abundance.

The grasslands of the desert overflow:
The hills are clothed with gladness.
The meadows are covered with flocks
and the valleys are mantled with grain;
They shout for joy and sing."

Acts 14:17 "He has shown kindness by giving you rain from heaven and crops in their seasons; He provides you with plenty of food and fills your hearts with joy." NIV.

But the blessing of rain is withheld because of the sin of the people of the land, eg Deut 11:17. (If you do not keep His commandments)...."Then the Lord's anger will burn against you, and *He will shut the heavens so that it will not rain* and the ground will yield no produce, and you will soon perish from the good land the Lord is giving you." NIV.

The earth itself responds. Hos 2:21 "In that day I will respond", declares the Lord "I will respond to the skies, and they will respond to the earth; and the earth will respond to the grain". NIV.

Jeremiah writes about the great drought:

Jer 14:1-7 NIV:

"This is the word of the Lord to Jeremiah concerning the drought:

Judah mourns, her cities languish, they wail for the land,
and a cry goes up from Jerusalem.
The nobles send their servants for water;
They go to the cisterns but find no water.
They return with their jars unfilled; dismayed and despairing they cover their heads.
The ground is cracked because there is no rain in the land;
The farmers are dismayed and cover their heads.
(Pray, heads covered with prayer shawls)
Even the doe in the field deserts her newborn fawn because there is no grass.
Wild donkeys stand on the barren heights and pant like jackals.
Their eyesight fails for lack of pasture.

Although our sins testify against us,
O Lord, do something for the sake of Your name,
For our backsliding is great;
We have sinned against You."

v22 Do any of the worthless idols of the nations bring rain?
Do the skies themselves send down showers?
No, it is you, O Lord our God.
Therefore our hope is in You, for you are the One Who does all this."

You may quote Matt 5:45 "He sends rain on the just and on the unjust." This is true, God in His goodness does this, but He is sovereign, and when necessary He withholds the blessing of rain (from the just and unjust alike), and the land and people groan.

From the beginning of my Christian life the Lord has shown me when He wants prayer for rain. Because He asks me to pray, I know that His time is now.

This is how I "came to faith". One day I was reading my Bible, not even aware that there was a severe drought in the country, and came to the account in 2 Samuel 7:27 RSV. "For Thou, O Lord of hosts, the God of Israel, hast made this revelation to Thy servant saying 'I will build you a house' therefore Thy servant has found courage to pray this prayer to Thee."

When God promised David that He would give him a continuing 'house' on the throne of Judah, David said "Seeing that You have promised me a house, I have confidence to ask that You will do this" (build me a house).

2 Sam 7:28,29 "Thou art God, and Thy words are sure, and Thou hast promised this good thing to Thy servant, now therefore may it please Thee to bless......for Thou, O Lord God, hast spoken."

The Lord then showed me unmistakably "Pray for rain." That evening on TV News they were speaking of the severe drought, animals dying, crops ruined, dams empty, and I realised that the Lord's request "Pray for rain" was indeed true and urgent.

I knew that just as David was confident to pray his prayer because the Lord had shown him the outcome was certain, so the prayer for rain was equally as certain of fulfilment because He had asked me to pray it.

I was so sure He would send rain I told my Scripture Class the following day about the awful drought - little animals dying etc. "Would you like to pray for rain so that the grass will grow and the dams will fill with water etc?"

Of course the children (nine year olds) were thrilled to pray for rain, and I prayed silently "Thankyou Lord, this will be a great faith-builder for the children." Sure enough, we had such heavy falls in the country that week that in most areas they declared the drought broken. The children were ecstatic, could hardly wait for next Scripture lesson, all calling out "It rained, it rained" as I walked into the classroom. "Thankyou Lord, we really were able to praise You for that."

During the years many times He showed me to pray for rain. I'll just give five examples:

1) He woke me at about 3am to pray for rain. There was a severe drought over most of Australia. As I knelt and prayed, in the Spirit I had a wonderful assurance. I knew spiritually I was similar (at that moment) to Queen Esther, that I had been standing in the inner court. Esther 5:2 NIV:

> "When he saw Queen Esther standing in the court, he was pleased with her and held out to her the gold sceptre that was in his hand. So Esther approached and touched the tip of the sceptre. Then the King asked, 'what is it Queen Esther? What is your request? Even up to half the kingdom, it will be given you.'"

I knew that in the Spirit I had touched the gold sceptre, and that my request would be granted "Rain, wherever it is needed, to fill the dams, and break the drought, that people may give thanks and glory to You God, and many souls won for You."

It rained, heavy soaking rain all over the State, drought-breaking rain.

2) He gave me the scripture "Ask of Me rain in the time of the latter rain". Zech 10:1, and as I was praying a tune came to me from Psalm 65:

> "You care for the land and water it,

You enrich it abundantly,
You drench its furrows with showers,
You bless it abundantly.

The meadows are covered with flocks,
And the valleys are mantled with grain,
They shout for joy and sing,
To You for You care for the earth."
This is my "Rain Song."

As I prayed and played the song, and sang it, I was interceeding for rain.

Heavy rain followed.

3) Praying at another time for rain in this needy land of ours which so often is short of rain, I felt again I was speaking to Jesus in a close personal way, as His betrothed.

"My Jesus, I want You to send rain."

"My Ruth, I want to send Repentance."

Of course often He can't send rain because it cuts across what He is trying to do spiritually, seeking that we turn from our sins. 2 Chron 7:14:

"If My people, who are called by My name, will humble themselves and pray, and seek My face, and turn from their wicked ways, then will I hear from heaven, and will forgive their sin and heal their land."

When His people, the Christians, have a close relationship with him, the land will be healed, and those that dwell therein.

Repentance too is a gift. We should ask that He will grant the gift of Repentance.

4) Douglas and I visited Lord Howe Island. The island was experiencing a three months drought, water restrictions had been imposed. We prayed for rain, and looking upwards, with eyes closed, I could see heavy rain falling right onto my face, falling from

a height - such a strange feeling.

Two days later there was so much rain the restrictions were lifted. Thankyou Lord.

5) I noticed a piece of paper lying under the bed, and couldn't seem to pick it up. Normally there's nothing difficult about picking up a slip of paper, but this seemed almost stuck to the floor.

After four or five attempts I knew there was something special about the words on the other side, turned it over, to read "Ask of Me rain, in the time of the latter rain."

"Yes Lord, there must be a drought again."

A day or two later a young girl from Wee Waa came for counselling. She said she was staying temporarily in Sydney because she'd been ill, and couldn't stand the moans and groans of the cattle, and calves on their property. They had four hundred and fifty head of cattle, with no feed and practically no water in the dams.

Together we prayed for rain, and two days later her mother rang her to say they'd had two and a half inches of rain that night, and the dams were half full. Thankyou Lord God, You are a wonderful prayer-answering God. I said I would write to their local paper and tell them the story, but have failed to do this. Please forgive me Lord, and let people from Wee Waa read this book and give You the glory.

2 Chron 7:14 "If My people......will humble themselves and pray."

Take Your glory Lord.

# Chapter 26
# **Further Back Healing**

A well-known Pastor with a healing ministry, Martin Morelli, was ministering at Bondi, and we went for further healing.

My back was so delicate I was concerned. I seemed to be having pain in three areas of the spinal column and neck, with the potential for sudden pain so severe I couldn't move for some seconds. I also had pain in the ball-joint of the foot.

Martin Morelli called for the people who were in pain when they entered the auditorium, and I went out for the pain in my foot. Martin was walking along the healing line when he had a 'Word of Knowledge', turned back to me and said "Sister, if you'll only believe, your back will be healed tonight." (I'd gone out for my foot, he couldn't have known about my back, it was a word from the Lord.) He laid hands on me and I was 'slain in the Spirit' and fell to the floor.

For six weeks after this, at least a dozen times a day I would feel a vibrant tingling hot patch on the left buttock, just where I sat down. It was a lovely feeling (winter time), almost as though I'd sat on a hot-water bottle. My back has been marvellous ever since, four years have passed, and it is now better than it has been for thirty years I'd say. Praise Jesus for his healings, and for living in Divine Health.

# Chapter 27
# The Burma (or Death) Railway

On 3rd May, 1983, a documentary film on the building of the Death Railway was screened on TV. James and Annie came to watch the film with us. I was appalled and most moved at what we saw.

How can we begin to know or understand the anguish and sacrifice of the men who built the Bridge over the River Kwai, who bled and agonised and died constructing the Death Railway, from the River Kwai to Burma?

Only those who took part, and can still hear the cries of their dying comrades, who can still see the pitiful forms of the mates they loved, emaciated and desperate, struggling for survival, death their constant companion, only they can understand.

Amongst the Australian boys taken when Singapore fell to the Japanese in 1942 was Bob Halliday, my late husband. He rarely spoke of his Prisoner of War experiences, particularly the tortures, which no doubt were indelibly etched in his memory, but I recall some of the experiences he shared with me.

His best friend, Bill Paterson, was taken prisoner with him. I asked Bill to give us a short account of their time spent working on the Railway. The following is an extract of his account:

# a) Bob Halliday - A Friend in Need

"I first met Bob Halliday in 1933 at Kogarah Primary School. I was a very timid twelve year old from the country, and his natural self-assurance helped me greatly in coping with my new environment. Little then did I know how much this friendship would influence my life, a friendship I still treasure, a friendship beyond understanding......

At the outbreak of war in 1939, enlistment for service overseas not only appeared right, but promised adventure too......

Our units were in camp at Rosebery Racecourse, and we embarked together from there on 15th July, 1941, knowing that we were going to Malaya to join an advance party of 8th Division who had left in February......

Our camps in Johore were just a few miles apart and we were able to keep in touch. We spent a memorable three day leave in Singapore in November 1941, staying at the Adelphi Hotel and living it up. How often we spoke of that leave later on......

After the Japanese attack on Singapore we were each busy in different areas and nine disastrous weeks later it was with relief that I located Bob after our sad trek out to Selarang Barracks at Changi. We camped in separate cottages only a few hundred yards apart.

Thus we began our three and a half years of incarceration.

The story of the unendurable sufferings and hardships of P.O.W.'s under the Japanese has been told many times. The recurrent story of mateship played a major role in survival. There were periods when through illness, we were separated, but we each had unit mates to and for support.

After a short period at Changi we went into

Singapore on work parties. Bob went to the Golf Course area, road building, and I to Bulit Timah. We returned to Changi in December '42 and apart from minor vitamin-related problems we were both reasonably fit.

In February '43 we left together on 'D' force for Thailand. We had now spent a year in captivity and that was enough. The next year was to be our real trial.

Our journey from Singapore to Banpong, Thailand, packed in enclosed steel railway trucks with little food and water was horrific. Just days later we began our real work at Kinsia (Kin Sai Yok). Bob did not look well, and despite our decision to boil our own drinking water each evening after work, and to practice strict hygiene, we both developed Dysentry. Bob was severely affected. I visited Bob in the sick hut when not working, and did all I could at the time. I made the mistake of lending him a book I had carried from Singapore - like Bob, it got thinner and thinner.

At this time, and only a short time after Bob had taken ill, all the 'fit' members of our original party were moved up to Bangon, about 35 miles North ......I was not to see Bob for nine months.

The monsoonal rains were just commencing and the memory of that period will not go away. I still feel the cold of the driving rain, and sense the mud underfoot, the discomforts of recurrent attacks of Malaria, and the unclean feeling of Dysentry......We lost more than half of our group at Bangon.

In February '44, after stumbling progress down the river through various camps, I was herded once more through the gates of the camp at Banpong where we had first entered the Siamese scene. I had lost all of my gear, including my treasured photos and letters. I owned a lap-lap as clothing, a large size tea-spoon and the small half of an army dixie. I was miserable, had reached the depths of despair, and was ready to give up as I had seen others do.

Entering the camp I had nodded to a few fellows I recognised, when I heard a strong voice say "Where have you been?" It was Halliday. Divine intervention, call it what you will, but at that moment I knew that we would survive. My spirits soared. I was washed, fussed over and Bob found me a real pair of shorts......

In mid-October we were separated again, until we were released almost a year later......

My mind often turns to that fateful weekend in '57 (Bob's death in the Aircrash), but more often I thank God for that brotherhood I was privileged to share, and the memories I retain."

Bill Paterson.

## b) Bob's Story

Bob said one of the worst experiences of his life was throwing his rifle onto the great heap of weapons just after Singapore fell. From that time he and his mates were helpless. He swore that if ever he were in a similar predicament he would use all his bullets on the enemy, except the last, which he'd use on himself. It was a dreadful thing to be taken prisoner, Bob said.

The prisoners were first housed in Changi Prison Camp on Singapore Island, many later being transferred up the Railway Line to work on the construction of this urgent project which the Japanese had been told would take five years, but which they forced men to death to build in eighteen months! The River Kwai Bridge was part of this Railway, thence through the jungle to Burma. Many British P.O.W.'s were building from Burma through Thailand to join up with the northward thrust.

The prisoners leaving Changi were promised better conditions, comfortable camps in the jungle, but the horrible truth was that they were shipped, in enclosed steel railway trucks, to a living hell. The further north they went the worse the conditions became.

The Japanese consider it a disgrace to be taken P.O.W. In their culture, their ethic, it is more honourable to die, so they had very little compassion on our men, working them often twelve hours a day on little more than a handful of polished rice. Many men developed beri-beri through lack of green vegetables and vitamins, and Bob said his section lived for a time on hibiscus leaves from a nearby hedge, boiling the leaves to add to the rice, making hibiscus soup. They also had a very distressing complaint called "Happy feet", caused by vitamin deficiency, where the men could not sit still, or lie down at night, because of the tingling in their feet, but paced up and down for hours on end, even though desperately tired from heavy work.

Bob used to sing a song chanted by the men as they were pile-driving. Japanese words for one, two, three sound something like "itchy, nee, sen" and the chant used was "itchy, nee, nesiah, nesiah," and on the second "nesiah" the men were to let the rope go, the weight fell, and the pile driven into the mud. Bob said the trouble was that one never knew how many "nesiahs" the Japanese soldier in charge would call (sometimes one, sometimes two, or at other times three). Confusion often reigned.

When our men were first taken captive they still had their unbroken Australian humour, and I have no doubt that with many it endured to the end. The

Japanese would line the men up, and make them number off - "One, two, three - itchy, nee, sen". Our men would say "Itchy, nee, scratchy!" "No, No!" "Start again!"

Bob developed Bacilliary Dysentry and his weight dropped from about thirteen stone to six and a half, pitifully thin as he was over six feet in height. He spoke of his life being saved by his buddy Bill Paterson, whose story is included here. He spoke of nursing Cholera and working in the Death House (Hospital) etc. after injuring his back on the railway.

He spoke of the inhuman tortures by the Japanese guards, men being kicked to death, filled with water and jumped on to burst their stomach or spleen (already distended with Malaria), the devastation of tropical ulcers eating into legs, leading to amputation (without anaesthetic), or death by gangrene. Many men died because they just didn't want to live any more.

There were stories of heroism, men giving their lives for their friends, and other stories of "the law of the jungle" taking over, men sinking to stealing from the dying etc. Here was anguish, despair, hopelessness, death, to an extent that we living in this affluent country could never comprehend.

But here, in the midst of death, was life!

## c) JESUS - The Answer

The real "Miracle on the River Kwai" was found in those men who reached out to Someone greater than . themselves, to the living Jesus Who Himself suffered, bore the rejection of men, scourging by the Roman whip, under which many died before they even reached the cross.

Reaching out to this Jesus, the Lover of men, Who laid down His own life that they might live, was real salvation. Here was a God Who suffered with men, not just a "Pie in the Sky when you die" God, but the Captain of our salvation, made perfect by suffering, One Who has gone before and Who bore it all, and Who understands.

Many men turned to Jesus, and in the sweet savour of His love, spent themselves untiringly for their fellows, encouraged, washed, fed others, doing without themselves. Strengthened by the Holy Spirit and the compassion of Jesus, they lived in the Secret Kingdom of a spiritual oneness with God.

These are the men who have been able to live or die victoriously over the tragedy of the Burma Railway, where it is said there was a dead man for every sleeper. These men can even forgive their Japanese torturers because they have learned to live in the love of Christ Who said to His Father from the cross "Father forgive them, for they know not what they do."

Bob survived the three years' captivity. He told me of the wonderful release from death which happened just after the capitulation of the Japanese. He was in a camp in the jungle, and the men had been ordered to dig a deep pit right around the camp. They were actually digging their own graves. All men were to stand beside the ditch and the Japanese intended to shoot them all and fill in the ditch. Any attempting to escape would be shot.

Fortunately for the prisoners an unexpected thing happened. Out of the blue, as it were, a British Officer and his Sergeant were parachuted into the Camp. The Officer carried a revolver at his hip, but the Sergeant behind him held a machine gun. The Officer asked to see the Japanese Commander in charge, and simply said "The war is over, you are all my prisoners, throw down your arms in a pile here at my feet". Covered by the Machine Gun they did!

I invited James and Annie to watch the documentary film on the building of the Burma Railway with us, thinking we might see the Dad whom he hadn't seen since he was three, but it was a vain hope. We saw Singapore, its fall, the Bridge over the Causeway and the British Regiment marching across, the rear guard being the Scottish Highland Band playing the pipes.

Bob told me that after the last man crossed, the British blew up the Causeway, still believing Singapore could never be taken, but this was comparatively easy, as all the heavy guns were pointed out to sea, Malaya being normally a peaceful hinterland.

Bemused by the scenes in Thailand, most of which had been shot some forty years previously, and greatly moved by the privation and anguish we had just witnessed, I was quite unprepared for the following news.

## d) James and Annie, Missionaries to Malaysia

After the film, when we were enjoying a cup of tea, James and Annie dropped the bombshell. They had been asked by our Church (Christian Life Centre, Darlinghurst), to be missionaries to Malaysia. I was dumbfounded!

Later the amazing timing began to unfold in my mind and heart - the film depicting Bob's war service and anguish in Singapore, Malaya, Thailand being shown two days before his (Bob's) birthday, James and Annie present, and that they were shortly to be sent to the lands shown on the map just seen on TV.

The Holy Spirit showed that in some wonderful way, James, bearing the Gospel of Peace, would help spiritually appease the hatred and killing and war and death in these lands where his father also walked, a prisoner, desolate. James would be carrying the Good News of the healing love of Jesus.

The Lord had already spoken to James and asked if he would "give his life for Him", and I had to come to grips with this thought too. He gave me Psalm 102:28 "The children of your servants will continue, and their descendants will be established before you."

As the days wore on, however, I was finding it increasingly hard to part with James. The Father showed me that he didn't want to part with Jesus either, He didn't say "Tra la la, off You go Jesus". He found it difficult to let Him go, it really cost the Father so much to send His Son. As someone said "God had only one Son, and He became a foreign missionary." Jesus had to go through much suffering, but He returned 'bringing His sheaves with Him." Yes Father, we love You, You gave Your precious Son to die that we might have life."

Doug and I saw them off at the Airport. It reminded me of something Bob's mother said to me after his fatal accident. "Bob came to say goodbye, and then turned and waved as he walked away - right out of my life." I buried my head in Doug's shoulder and cried, I just couldn't watch James leave.

James and Annie left for Malaysia on 15th June, '83 sent out with prayer and prophecy, by the Holy Spirit, and the Church.

# Chapter 28
# Feast of Tabernacles

Doug and I were hoping to attend the Christian Feast of Tabernacles in Jerusalem, praying about it, and on my birthday in June the Lord gave the "all clear" to go. In fact, He said to me through the Holy Spirit "This is your birthday present from Me." We learned wonderful things in Jerusalem that year.

The Feast of Tabernacles is celebrated at the time of the ingathering of the harvest, one of the three feasts that are compulsory for the Jews to celebrate. Lev 23:42, Deut 16:16.

It is a magnificent experience to attend the Christian Feast, a week of singing, dancing, praising God, fellowship and listening to wonderful Christian teachers from the far ends of the earth. Interestingly enough, the Jews call this celebration the "Messiah's Feast."

Forty three nations joined in the Praise Walk down the Mount of Olives, following the route taken by Jesus as He descended the steep, slippery path, crossed the brook Kidron and entered the City of Jerusalem as King. Zech 9:9.

"Rejoice greatly O daughter of Zion, shout, O daughter of Jerusalem: behold your King is coming to you, he is just and having salvation, lowly and riding on a donkey, a colt, the foal of a donkey."

We gathered near the Western Wall (sometimes referred to as the Wailing Wall), and the leader of International Christian Embassy, Jerusalem addressed the

Jews, repenting on behalf of Christian persecution of the Jews over the centuries.

## a) Release of the Soviet Jews

On another occasion the forty three nations marched through the streets of Jerusalem for release of the Soviet Jews. We carried banners "You are not alone Israel", "Comfort My people" and various demands for release of the Jews such as "Let My people go". We sang "Shalom Alakem" and Christian choruses as we marched, waving and calling "Shalom". The people accepted us, blew kisses and thanked us for caring.

One of the speakers on the plight of the Jews in the USSR was Abraham Shiffrin, who spent twenty nine days in a cupboard, feet frozen in mud and urine, ankle deep. He slept on the ice, and later lost a foot. As a Jew he had refused to integrate in the "wonderful Russian people".

There are literally thousands of Concentration Slave Labour Camps in USSR, where hundreds of thousands die each year, mainly slaving in the Uranium Mines (without protective clothing), and working on the overland natural gas line. They labour twelve hours a day, often in sub-zero temperatures with little food.

Psychiatric Hospitals and Prisons are also places of torture, violence and death. Many of the Jews are in prison, accused, often falsely, as the Christians also are, of being "trouble makers". They are considered undesirables because they will not bow to the Communist System. The Russians say they must be mad if they don't accept the Communist system, and put them in Psychiatric Hospitals. They may also be classified as trouble makers and incarcerated in Prisons or Slave

Labour Camps, on trumped-up charges.

The "Refuseniks" (Jews who have applied for release to live in Israel, and refused), are immediately dismissed from their jobs, and persecuted. However, the Scriptures show that the Jews will return to Israel from all over the world, including the USSR.

The Lord began to show me his plans for Israel, and this new outlook has changed my life.

Jer 30: 3,10:

"The days are coming", says the Lord, "that I will bring back from captivity My people Israel and Judah, and I will cause them to return to the land that I gave to their fathers and they shall possess it.

I will save you from afar, and your seed from the land of their captivity. Jacob shall return, have rest, and be quiet, and no one shall make him afraid."

Zech 14:9:

"And the Lord" (the returned Messiah) "shall be King over all the earth."

# b) The Second Exodus

Is 43:5,6 (The return of the Jews to their land)

"I will bring your descendents from the East and gather you from the West. I will say to the North 'give up' and to the South 'Do not keep them back', bring My sons from afar, and My daughters from the ends of the earth."

Jer 16:14,15:

"Therefore behold, the days are coming, says the Lord, that it shall no more be said, "The Lord lives, Who brought up the children of Israel from the land of Egypt, *but the Lord lives Who brought up the children of Israel from the land of the North and from all the lands where He had driven them, for I will bring them back into their land which I gave to their fathers."* Also Jer 23: 7,8, Jer 31, especially v8, 32:36-44, Ezek 36.

There are almost the same number of Israelites in USSR as there were in Egypt when Moses led them, by the Holy Spirit, to Israel. As expressed in the verses above, the second Exodus will be greater than the first; this will be really something, as every Jew religiously celebrates Passover, the Exodus from Egypt, each year. God says He will be known as the Lord of the Second Exodus.

And the Exodus has already begun.

# Chapter 29
# The Return of the Jews to Israel

If a man is healed does is affect the nations? If a man is raised from the dead, do they believe? The answer is "No", BUT, the restoration of the Jews to Israel is a practical issue that may be seen and demonstrated. Jesus will rule the nations from Jerusalem, and God will be glorified in the eyes of all the nations upon earth. Marxism says, "There is no God", Islam says, "Allah is God, and Mahomed is his prophet." Around the Dome of the Rock, the Islamic Mosque on the Temple Mount, are written these words "Allah is God, he has no son, worship God alone."

"HE HAS NO SON!" We will see. God is about to prove them wrong, by this tiny nation of Israel. "Israel is so small', says Amos 7:2,5, and she is surrounded by millions of hostile people. The population of Israel is nearly four million, the Soviets two hundred and sixty million and Islamic nations surrounding Israel, one hundred and ten million. Israel must look to the Lord as she looked to Him in the time of Balaam's visit to Barak. Num 24:5.

"How lovely are your tents O Jacob, and your dwellings O Israel". (They were outnumbered by countless hordes of Midianites at the time.) God will use Israel to break the spirit of Islam and confound atheism before the whole world.

Prophecy is being fulfilled. The Jews are returning to their land. Over 180,000 Iraqui Jews, most Iranian Jews, all Yemeni and most North African Jews

234

have returned to Israel. Of those in Ethiopia (generally called the Falashas, although I believe this is a derogatory term, and I ask pardon for using it), almost half have been flown to Israel.

We need to pray for the remaining Jews to return to Israel as it is part of God's plan. It is here they will recognise the Messiah when He returns, and the 'remnant' of Israel will be saved.

Even though the Scriptures warn of the USSR sweeping down into the land, and nuclear war, the Jews are still urged to return, as it is in the land of Israel that they will meet their Messiah. Jerusalem will supplant the United Nations in that day, and the whole world will "go up to Zion" to worship King Jesus.

God is at present calling the Jews to go up to Zion willingly, according to the scripture Jer 16:16:

"Behold, I will send for many fishermen, says the Lord, and they shall fish them, and afterward I will send for many hunters, and they shall hunt them from every mountain and every hill, and out of the holes of the rocks."

The Jews are mostly being gently asked by the fishermen to return to their land, but when the time of the fishermen is fulfilled, He will send for many 'hunters'. This is the coming expected rise of anti-semitism throughout the world, when the nations of the earth will expel them and they will be hunted back to Israel.

I didn't at first see the significance of this setting up of Israel again as the national land of the Israelites, but the Lord opened my eyes after this third visit to Israel, and I saw many things.

  1. That I was called to intercede for the Jews, and this call dated back to 1959 when I was first saved. I believe we can be missionaries on the

wings of prayer to the Jewish people.

2. The Messiah will not return to an empty Israel. He has given the Promised Land to His people and the 'redeemed remnant' will be those who believe His promise (even though it is just a stirring in their heart), and act on their faith, and the faith of their fathers, by returning to the land.

3. As in the days of the Babylonian captivity only those who had a heart after God returned. The others wouldn't leave their Babylonian businesses, families, luxurious homes, good schools, swimming pools etc. Only those who returned received the promises of God.

4. Even though Russia will come down into Israel, the Promised Land is the safest place for a Jew in the world today, eg. Nazi Germany and the Holocaust.

5. In Genesis we have the Creation story. In order to create, God spoke. Gen 3:1, "And God SAID, let there be light, and there was light." God SPOKE the whole creation into being, but in the last days He will "ROAR" out of Zion. Joel 3:16, Amos 1:2, Jer 25:30, and the whole earth will tremble before the God of Abraham, the God of Isaac and the God of Jacob.

6. I marvel at the return to Israel of the Falasha tribe (Beta Israel.) Over the years I have prayed for revival in this Tribe, and wondered at the incredible airlift of so many of these precious souls to Tel Aviv. I believe they will be amongst those who accept Jesus as Messiah and are saved. Praise God for His ways, past finding out.

7. I believe all Christians should be praying that the Gospel be preached to every tongue, tribe, nation and people. Equally important is the return of the Jews to their land. Until these two missions

are accomplished the return of the Messiah is being held back.

Christians, love the Jews, uphold and comfort them. Accept them for what they are, our brothers and sisters in the Lord. Pray for their salvation for the Lord has plans for Jew and Christian.

According to the promises given to Abraham, Gen 22:17, for the Christians, as the stars of the sky, there is a heavenly plan. We are a spiritual people. It is our responsibility to pray for the Jews. As the sand of the sea, the Jews are earthly people, who are identified with the land, the Promised Land. Their destiny is earthy, that through them God will be glorified in Israel. He will be glorified in Jerusalem, the City of our God, before the nations of the earth, and then the Israelites will recognise their Messiah and be saved. Hallelujah! Zech 12:10 "They will look upon me Whom they have pierced;...they will mourn..." John 19:37.

God will judge the nations according to how they have treated His people. Joel 3:3, Matt 25:31-46:

"Inasmuch as you did it to one of the least of these My brethren you did it to Me," says Jesus.

Let us uphold Israel in every way. Ps 122:6-9:

"Pray for the peace of Jerusalem: may they prosper who love you. Peace be within your walls, prosperity within your palaces. For the sake of my brethren and companions, I will now say 'Peace be within you'. Because of the house of the Lord our God I will seek your good."

The highlight of our visit to Israel this time was a re-dedication in the River Jordan. Doug and I had both been christened as babies. We were also baptised as adults in the Lane Cove River, separately, but now we went down into the waters of baptism together as man and wife. This ceremony is actually a burial, the burying of the old man of sin and rising a new creature from the grave in resurrection life, as Jesus did.

The Jordan teams with little fish, which nibbled our toes as we stood in the water. The old Douglas and Ruth are buried in Israel.

And is there a special way to pray for Israel? Yes!

The prayer the Lord gave me for Israel was a very simple one. "Ask of me rain, at the time of the latter rain." Zech 10:1. Pray for precious rain, physical and spiritual, without which Israel would perish, but praise God, He is sending it.

# Chapter 30
# We Visit the Burma Railway

Leaving Israel we flew to Britain and after visiting relatives and friends on to Amsterdam. From there we flew to Bangkok, where we caught a bus to the River Kwai Village. Here are some thoughts written at that time:

"Rain, rain, rain. A steady unrelenting downpour. Little streams gushed along the gutters and overflowed into the already saturated fields on either side of the road. On and on our bus bumped and splashed. Suddenly a large black signboard, "The River Kwai Hotel Village." We drove under a barrier lifted mechanically by an attendant seated in a box out of the rain. The bus then turned sharply downwards as we saw the roofs of the hotel beside the brown muddy waters of the Kwai River, swollen by heavy rains.

This was the wet season. Sometimes the rain would ease, then sweep up the valley in a white turbulent rush. Bangkok was in flood.

And why am I here?

Because my heart goes out to the boys who worked, and perhaps died, on the Railway. Many of these boys lie in unmarked graves here in the jungle. I shed a tear as I remembered the message on a tombstone I saw at the War Cemetery. A young Scottish boy buried there with the plaintive message on a wooden cross, "Lying here in a foreign land, please place a flower for me, Mum."

The atmosphere here is heavy, dark, oppressive,

forbidding, sultry, despairing. I hear the cry of our men in my heart, dying bewildered, "Why me, God, why me? I'm so young, too young to die, and all alone."

The following day we swept down the river in a small boat with long outboard motor. We sped along beside logs and small trees, bamboo, rubbish, all the flotsam that sweeps down a river in flood - arriving at our destination, the Death Railway.

We waited beside the track for an hour or more. No one seemed impatient, they were quite used to the timelessness of this eastern land. We eventually boarded the long overdue train.

At first we travelled along flat country, the mountains dividing Thailand and Burma relatively close. Then we slowed our pace as the track began winding along the high side of the river. The original tracks etc. were still those laid by the prisoners, but these have been bolstered now by additional steel supports, where the track is partly supported by scaffolding. I was pleased to see the additional bracing, as I'd read accounts in Ernest Gordon's "Miracle on the River Kwai" of white ants being introduced by the prisoners, struts cut off just below the surface of the ground etc., I wondered if at any moment we would plunge into the muddy waters below.

And why was I here? Because I loved Bob and longed to enter into this part of his life, to somehow share the trauma and heartache of it all. "Deep calleth unto deep".

Will we see our loved ones again? Are they with Jesus? I know by what the Lord showed me regarding my mother's death, that it is quite possible for the dying soul to have an encounter with Jesus, when He, in His great love, may speak with them and explain to them the truths of Kingdom, hidden in the blindness of their earthly life. This may especially happen when prayers are being said for them by believing loved ones. I don't believe all our prayers go for nothing. Time stands still for God when He so desires. He is the Lord of time. All life in the spiritual realm stands still while our Lord speaks.

I know that Jesus has such great love for His people that He would have spoken to many of these young men. They were no doubt bewildered in the face of death, puzzled and hurt that they had not yet really lived, and that they were dying away from their loved ones. How precious it would have been to speak to them of Jesus at this time, to say softly "The Lord is my Shepherd, I shall not want," and lead them beside the still waters to a knowledge of the Saviour. These thoughts and many more filled my heart as we travelled over the Railway which claimed so many lives.

Lord I believe it was not in vain. "O Love, that will not let me go, I rest my weary soul in Thee". I believe that many are with You, Lord. What a Saviour!

Bangkok was so flooded we didn't even know if we'd make it to the Airport. The water in the canals was higher than the road, but thank God we reached the Airport. We flew down to Kuala Lumpur, where James and Annie were waiting for us.

Great to see them, stay a few days, eat Malaysian and Chinese food and bathe Malaysian style with dippers of water.

The Church was strong and growing, with a Chinese Pastor in charge, who took us out for a real Chinese meal. Thankyou Sunny!

From Kuala Lumpur we travelled by train to Singapore, and on taking off from the Airport, I was able to catch a glimpse of Changi Prison, where Bob spent some time as Prisoner of War. We flew by Qantas home to Sydney.

## a) Benaiah James

James and Annie returned after only five months missionary service in Malaysia because they were unable to renew their visas. James was appointed Assistant Pastor at the Christian Life Centre, Liverpool, and on the twenty fourth of September '84, Annie gave birth to Benaiah James, their first child.

The Lord gave His blessing. Doug's morning reading was from Haggai 2:10,18,19,23:

> v10 "On the twenty fourth day of the ninth month (today's date, twenty fourth September), the word of the Lord came….
>
> v18 Consider now, from this day forward, from the twenty fourth day of the ninth month, ….consider it.
>
> v19….from this day forward I will bless you.
>
> v23….and I will make you as a signet ring; for I have chosen you, says the Lord of hosts."

What a wonderful blessing for a little boy. Benaiah in the Bible was one of David's "Mighty Men".

The Lord gave me a song (with tune) for him from 1 Chronicles 11:22:

> "Benaiah is a man of God,
> Benaiah is a man of God,
> He slew a lion in a pit
> On a snowy day."

# Chapter 31
# Guidance or Divination?

Guidance can be such a problem to many Christians as we seek to walk in the Spirit. How do we know His will?

Doug and I needed to make an important "Yes" or "No" decision. I prayed, but didn't seem to receive any guidance, and finally in exasperation decided to ask for a specific answer from the Word.

For years Jesus used to answer me from the Bible. I had only to kneel in prayer, ask for guidance, open the Word and read, and the answer was right there almost every time, when I was close to Him.

I also remember one awful occasion when I was backsliding. I knew in my heart that I was not in fellowship with Him, and that I was presumptious asking Him to pay any attention to my prayer, but decided to ask anyway.

"Lord, I just want a "Yes" or "No" answer. I read the Bible, and received nothing. "Lord, I'll flip through the pages till I come to either something positive or negative like 'Yea, thus saith the Lord' for yes, or 'No, I will not....' for no."

I flipped through the Bible, seeing nothing negative or positive, (a miracle in itself), and then He gave me a scripture, Job 37:20 NEB:

"Can a man dictate to God when He is to speak, or command Him to make proclamation?"

In other words He would not answer me, nor be tricked into giving me a negative or a positive (make proclamation?). I was chastened and unhappy. I knew I was out of fellowship, but foolishly was not at this time repentant enough or broken enough to turn back.

I also remembered the good times we had together when He spoke to me daily.

In the period in the wilderness before I was baptised in the Holy Spirit, He mainly spoke to me through the Word.

After the infilling of the Holy Spirit, I knew in my heart that He now wanted me to be led by the Spirit, to walk in the Spirit in a deeper way. I was no longer permitted to kneel and open the Bible for an answer in black and white. This could become divination, and I knew it.

Doug and I now needed an answer and I knelt and prayed hesitantly saying "Lord, I know You stopped me dipping into the Word for an answer, but I can't seem to hear the voice of the Spirit in this matter. I'll open the Word, and read. If I'm doing the wrong thing please show me, I wouldn't dare open myself up to a spirit of divination."

I opened the Bible, and came to Ezek 21:21:

"For the King of Babylon stands at the parting of the road, at the fork of the two roads, to use *divination*. He shakes the arrows, he consults the images, he looks at the liver.

v22 At his right hand is the *divination* for Jerusalem......

v23 and it will be to them as a false *divination*."

Lord I get the message. As someone pointed out, He graciously answered me by the very means He was warning me against. As we grow in the Spirit, we must learn to hear and recognise His voice. John 10:27:

"My sheep hear My voice", says Jesus.

He revealed His answer to us by circumstances falling into place and a peace in our hearts.

# Chapter 32
# Christ in You - The Hope of Glory

I have been conscious that my heart was "Lukewarm", and I wanted the fire of love in my heart for Jesus. How hurtful if we asked someone "Do you love me?" and they said, with a shrug, "I suppose so, yes, I guess I do" in an offhand, half-hearted way with a barely disguised yawn. This is often the temperature of our love for Jesus, and He says "I'll spue you out of My mouth." (Meaning "you are an offence to Me, you make Me sick".)

I had been asking the Holy Spirit to help me fall deeply in love with Jesus. Jesus revealed to me that the reason my love had cooled off that I was thinking of Him "Up there" with the Father, whereas the Word also says "Christ *in* you, the hope of glory."

Jesus is at the right hand of the Father, but if we only see Him there, and direct our prayer up there to Him, He becomes impersonal to us. He is up there, but He is also in here, within, and it is as we acknowledge Him within, closer than breathing, that our love for Him grows warmer.

As I spoke to Jesus within, loved Him within, my love began to burn. The Spirit showed me that our relationship with Jesus is three fold. He is:

1) Seated at the right hand of the Father, or the Lamb in the midst of the throne, in glory, to be worshipped.

2) Brother, Betrothed, Friend, Redeemer, the

Crucified One, now Resurrected and walking with us in the form of a Man.

3) Jesus within, closer than breathing.

Shortly after this realisation, I was walking along the street, and suddenly received a tremendous shock! *Jesus was looking out of my eyes.* Incredulous at first, I then thought "I'll look at people as He sees them," and almost immediately the feeling was gone, and I didn't think of it again for days. (The birds of the air snatch up the seed!)

Then I felt He showed me that He was indeed within, and that He didn't want to just look out of my eyes, but He wanted to inhabit my whole body. I thought "Lord, if You want Your mind in my mind, I can't think any ungodly thoughts otherwise You'll be uncomfortable there. Lord, if Your heart is to be in my heart, I must have a heart of compassion like Yours, otherwise You will be unhappy there. Lord, if Your ears are in my ears they must only listen to and accept what You would want to hear. Lord, if Your hands are in my hands, mine being just a glove as it were for Yours, what a difference it will make to my ministry. I'll lay hands on the sick, and they'll always be instantly healed, delivered, strengthened. I must believe for it.

Walking up and down one morning praising and praying, I suddenly felt Jesus within again. This time I seemed to grow very large, to almost reach the ceiling. The chairs etc. all seemed quite small and I knew that this Jesus within was supremely powerful. It wouldn't matter what disaster happened, Jesus is Master of it, completely in control.

Then I slowly spiritually shrank back to normal size.

On another occasion He reminded me that He'll be coming back, and I will stand face to face with Him.

He said "Will you be comfortable gazing into My eyes? Will you be able to return My gaze?

Will we be able to gaze into His all-seeing eyes and say "Lord, I love You", or will we, like many, call on the rocks to hide us from the face of the Lamb? "Beloved, if our heart does not condemn us, we have confidence toward God." 1 John 3:21.

The very thought of being able to look into His eyes without shame is challenging. I did see His eyes once in a vision, as He turned and looked at me. I have never seen anything more beautiful in my whole life, but there is nothing, absolutely nothing, hidden from His gaze. His magnificent eyes penetrate like laser beams, but totally pure, totally true, totally loving, completely unhurried, absolutely in command. Words fail me.

Jesus is indeed in us, and if we could only take hold of this truth in faith, and not allow Satan to snatch away the seed of belief and trust, our lives would be transformed. We would also find our love growing hot within us, because He is so real, so relevant, almost within our grasp. Keeping His commandments would be so much easier.

Unfortunately the birds of the air often snatch away the seed. We experience these great truths of the Christian life, walk in them for a while, and then they are replaced by something else, and often forgotten. Perhaps this is growth? Progress? How do we retain all these spiritual truths?

# Chapter 33
# Writing This Book

In my Quiet Time the Lord spoke regarding writing this book.

"To everything there is a season, and a time to every purpose under the heaven" Eccl 3:1, and this is the time to begin writing, the time I've looked forward to for years. I've had to wait until now to understand what it will be about, what Jesus wants to say.

He spoke to me from Daniel 4:2:

"I thought it good to declare the signs and wonders that the Most High God has worked for me."

It is a book of testimony.

He spoke to me from 1 Chronicles 28:

v10 "Consider now, for the Lord has chosen you to"....(write a book)...."be strong and do it."

v11 "Then David gave to his son Solomon the plans for....

v12 and the plans for all that he had by the Spirit,

v19 all this....the Lord made me understand in writing by His hand upon me, all the words of these plans."

A message from him like this gives hope and confidence, I am confident that this book is written in the Spirit, and by the Spirit will succeed in every way God plans. I was given this message two weeks before I began re-reading my spiritual diary.

As I reviewed my life, dating back to conversion in November 1957, the Lord showed me that the book was an appraisal of my life. It will be revealed as such, similar to Solomon looking at his life, and writing his memoirs in Ecclesiastes.

The conclusion Solomon came to at the end of his life is expressed in Ecclesiastes 12:13,14:

"Let us hear the conclusion of the whole matter. Fear God and keep His commandments, for this is the whole duty of man.

For God will bring every work into judgment, including every secret thing, whether it is good, or whether it is evil."

I believe it is also imperative to KNOW God, and to LOVE Him.

A well-known chorus comes to mind, Author unknown.

"The greatest thing in all my life
Is knowing You,
The greatest thing in all my life
Is knowing You.
I want to know You more, I want to know You more,
The greatest thing in all my life
Is knowing You.

The greatest thing in all my life
Is loving You,
The greatest thing in all my life,
Is loving You.
I want to love You more, I want to love You more,
The greatest thing in all my life
Is loving You.

The greatest thing in all my life
Is serving You,
The greatest thing in all my life
Is serving You.
I want to serve You more,
I want to serve You more,
The greatest thing in all my life
Is serving You.

# Chapter 34
# Living It All Again

I reminisce! I remember those sunsets in Russia and particularly the one going through the Ural Mountains. This was quite different from the earlier ones as the train plunged on through the forests of Southern Siberia. The trees would parade past on the run - a monotonous stream - with the sun sinking down towards their tops.

Now it is lower and behind them flashing intermittent streams of golden light, through the dark trees now in silhouette. Suddenly no more flashing; the sun has set, darkness taking over remorselessly.

But over the Urals, the trees did not come right up to the railway line except in clumps. Between the clumps we could see long vistas to a far distant setting sun. When the sun would finally go down behind distant mountains, the expanse in between would be instantly dark, contrasting against the bright sky. The clouds are golden turning to red, progressing to darker and darker red until finally it is night.

I meditate on the highlights of the years I have lived, and reluctantly consider the failures. I try to be honest with myself and look at these events dispassionately.

What is a life? What does it all mean?

Somehow it all seems like a dream, as though it never really happened. Today is real, yesterday is but a memory.

How will I feel when I stand before the Judgment Seat of Christ? Will I be ashamed, or will I be able to meet His steady gaze? His penetrating eyes will look deep into mine, and He will see all, everything, for exactly what it is. Initially I won't have to say a word. Then He will ask me to give an account of my life. Rom 14:12.

I stand on a high point at sixty four, reviewing the highlights of the years I have lived.

I consider that my real life only began thirty years ago when at 34½ I called out to God in despair and the Holy Spirit came into me, as described in the body of the book.

Jesus came into my life at this time and gave me "Zoe", God's eternal life. Zoe is quality, the kind of life God possesses, the kind of life that can live in heaven with Him forever.

The Christian life is "normal". Anything else is "sub-normal".

I recall my "sub-normal" years with a certain amount of regret. If only I had handed my life over to Jesus earlier - life without Him is empty, wasted. In case you should think I was a miserable soul before meeting Jesus let me show you what kind of person I was.

Born in Sydney in 1923, of loving parents who wanted a daughter, I was named "Evelyn" by my father and "Ruth" by my mother, generally known as "Ruthie".

I had a happy childhood although my relationship with my father was never a close cuddling one. He was proud of me, from a distance, but all I felt was rejection.

Educated in Church schools, I nevertheless became most rebellious - against parental authority, teachers and the Moderator of the Presbyterian Church, who sent me to the Headmistress for punishment after reading my scatty Scripture notes. Religion meant very little to me.

On leaving school I attended University and studied Science for two years. Rebelling against Uni and study I joined the Air Force as a WAAAF during the War. As a WAAAF I was rebellious and "did my own thing", like going AWL (Absent Without Leave), sleeping-in instead of going on parades etc.

On discharge from the WAAAF after the War finished I entered into a disastrous second engagement - (my first fiance was killed in a plane crash). My mother was distraught and encouraged my father to take me for a week's holiday in Tasmania. This was in order to establish a closer relationship with me and talk me into breaking the engagement.

The manouvre failed until my father applied pressure saying that if I married Martin he would sell up all his assets and move to South Africa. I would not be welcome in his house while I was married to this man.

My father also proved to me through a solicitor that this man I intended marrying was a wife-beater with an alcohol problem. I decided that I would be a fool to marry Martin, and broke the engagement. Four weeks later I met Bob. We fell in love and he wanted me to elope after we'd known one another one week. I was tempted to do this, but by this time was a little scared of my longsuffering father. I declined to run away with Bob - and how did I know that he would marry me anyway?

Six months later, Bob and I were married and eventually moved to Kangaroo Point. It was from this house that he left on his disastrous trip abroad, and his death. I see my life to this point as being without real purpose, stumbling around in the dark, as it were. With the brash self-reliance of youth I didn't give the future a thought.

I was accustomed to getting my way with the

strength of my own will. Standing on my own two feet was the answer to my problems.

Entering into marriage with Bob was an example of my self-determination. I thought "if it only lasts three years it will have been worth it. If the marriage doesn't last I'll divorce him and marry someone else - easy!" I was utterly selfish and self-centred. I also had a problem looming ahead in the form of alcohol.

During the War many of my friends became heavy drinkers. I belonged to the Sergeants Mess, which was a "wet mess". In other words alcohol was served. We sat around in the evening drinking beer for want of something better to do - singing and playing the piano. Drinking became part of my life.

Bob and I drank a lot in the evenings and during the weekends. I often had a kerosene tin of home brew on the kitchen sink from which I bottled a very cloudy, lively, highly potent beer. Alcohol was becoming a problem to me.

Then the Air Crash!

Then Jesus came into my life, bless His wonderful name. You've already read about it in this book. When the Holy Spirit came in power He transformed my life even further. Now I am learning to walk in the Spirit.

And how about you? Where do you stand?

Writing this book I have endeavoured to show my life before I found Jesus. I was in Egypt, (a land of bondage, a land where people lived and died without going anywhere - spiritually that is). Egypt represents the world, the kind of life lived by the average person. The people here are often lovely people, good living, generous and kind. Some may be far from good, but good or bad we all need Jesus. Jesus said "I am the Way, the Truth and the Life. No man comes to the Father but by Me." John 12:6.

You might be living a good life but unless you have opened your heart to Jesus you don't have "Zoe" life, God's kind of life. If you don't have "Zoe", you have no hope of going to heaven. You will spend eternal life in hell, to put it bluntly.

You say "I have received Jesus into my heart and life. I have "Zoe", God's eternal life, I am saved from hell fire and on my way to heaven." That's great, but think now about the second section of the book called "The Wilderness".

The people of God in the Old Testament were set apart to God in the wilderness, in which they wandered disillusioned, aimlessly for forty years. The reason they wandered so long in this dry, barren land was that the leaders disobeyed the Lord's command. God's promise was "I will take you to a land flowing with milk and honey, and will cast out the enemy before you." (My paraphrase.)

When the time came (some months after leaving Egypt), to enter the Promised Land, the leaders, through unbelief, said "there are giants in the land and the cities are walled. We can't possibly survive, we are like grasshoppers in their sight, and in our own sight."

They did not enter in because of unbelief!

The Promised Land is our full inheritance in Christ. God wants us to enter. Certainly there are giants, but we have the promise of the Father: Acts 1:10:

"You will receive power after the Holy Spirit has come upon you."

This promise is fulfilled in the Infilling or Baptism in the Holy Spirit when we become filled with the power of God. Power for fighting the enemy, power for witnessing, power for living the Spirit-filled life.

Have you received the Baptism in the Holy Spirit?

Have you received this power? It is available. It is yours for the asking.

Through the Baptism in the Holy Spirit you will find the gifts of the Spirit available to you:

"Word of Wisdom, Word of Knowledge, Discerning of spirits, Faith, Healings, Miracles, Prophecy, Tongues and Interpretation of Tongues".

It is through these gifts that we are enabled to fight the enemy in the Promised Land.

Do you want to be a "full-on" Christian? Then:

a) Receive Jesus as Saviour and Lord

b) Be baptised in the Holy Spirit

c) Be immersed in water as Jesus was

and go in His strength to walk in the Spirit.

This is my testimony - "He gave me life." How about you?

He changed me from a totally self-centred, wilful, rebellious, hurt person with a growing alcohol problem into the person I am today. I am certainly not perfect in myself, but I am learning, and growing into the person He wants me to be. My life has purpose. How about yours?

I see myself at 64 meditating on the highlights of the years I have lived. I see the world around me steadily plunging towards darkness. All around the skies are red and sombre.

I do not find myself heading towards a Russian sunset with its darkening remorse and finality. No. As the world around me gets darker, all I see ahead of me is a Sunrise. My new life dawned 30 years ago, and I find myself looking towards a brightening sky to the East.

Some day soon the sun will rise flooding its golden light all around me to an extent I cannot now comprehend. I shall find myself at last looking at my

Saviour. This I cannot comprehend either except that I know it will be.


## THE END


PS. To receive Jesus as Saviour just say a simple prayer like:

"Lord Jesus, I believe You died on the Cross for my sins. Please forgive me and come into my life. Make me the person You want me to be and lead me into the plan You have for my life.    Amen."


**For a full list of Sovereign World titles write to:**

P.O. Box 17, Chichester, West Sussex PO20 6RY, England
P.O. Box 329, Manly, N.S.W. 2095, Australia
P.O. Box 24086, Royal Oak, Auckland, New Zealand
14 Balmoral Road, Singapore 1025


**Crisis Call's address is:**

P.O. Box 236, St. Leonards, N.S.W. 2065, Australia
All pertinent correspondance will be answered.